Another in his 'day to day.

ALF STRANGE

Following Me Dad

Best wishes

alf Strange

GEE & SON LIMITED
DENBIGH, CLWYD

First Impression: November 15, 1986
Second Impression: November 25, 1986
Third Impression: September 1992

ISBN 0 7074 0114 3

By the same author:
'Me Dad's the Village Blacksmith'

First Impression: 1983
Ninth Impression: 1992

Printed and Published by
GEE & SON LIMITED, DENBIGH, CLWYD, WALES

Contents

INTRODUCTION

I WAS very honoured to be asked by my good friend Alf Strange to write an introduction to his first book called *Me Dad's the Village Blacksmith*, which has raised thousands of pounds for the Royal Shrewsbury Hospital.

Now he has found time to write his second book which he has called *Following Me Dad*.

In this book the author tells of life around his beloved Village of Welsh Frankton.

What memories it brings to me of my village of over forty years ago, when evacuees from Liverpool arrived, the Home Guard was formed and of all those old characters of the Village, many of whom regretfully have now passed on.

The author's wealth of memory of those pre-War and post-War years had me amazed when I read his latest script.

Everybody who loves true and humourous *Strange* stories of country life will be truly fascinated by this latest edition.

I, for one, fully recommend it.

GRAFTON BEDDOES.

Platt Farm,
Prees.

ACKNOWLEDGEMENTS

I WISH to record grateful thanks to my friend, Bernard Hallett for all his help, and to Iorwerth Roberts for his invaluable assistance during the preparation of this book.

My sincere thanks are due once again to the publishers, Gee and Son (Denbigh) Ltd. for all their help and guidance.

A.S.

October 1986.

PREFACE

IT is now more than seven years since I first put pen to paper to record some of the history of Frankton through the people and the characters I have known there during my life.

When I first started that self imposed task, I had no premonition at all of the effect it would have on my life, nor did I ever think I would achieve an unlikely ambition for a village blacksmith — putting his native village on the map.

Frankton has been my home since my birth on an October day in 1925, and I have had no desire to live anywhere else. When I wrote it, I hoped my first book *Me Dad's the Village Blacksmith* would be a success and that the money it raised would help to save someone's life in future, in exactly the way that the skill of doctors and the care of nurses at the Coronary Care Unit at the Royal Shrewsbury Hospital had saved my life.

I will forever be indebted to my own doctor for his skill and prompt attendance in the early hours of October 23, 1980. It meant I was in hospital in a very short time, taken there by reassuring ambulancemen whose kindness is still very vivid in my memory.

Those 16 days in hospital were traumatic, but to come out of hospital, to feel the rain on your face, to be able to walk again, to talk again with neighbours and friends, is another experience altogether. I will never again complain of trivial things. Life is too short, far too short to indulge in such inconsequentials, and I intend to make the most of the years I have left and to try and follow the advice of the old saying that it is 'better to wear out than rust out.'

7

This second book takes on the story, not merely of the Strange family of Blacksmiths, but of life in my little border village of Frankton through war, and rationing and agriculture revolution, as *I follow me Dad* in the leather apron on village blacksmith. Like my first book, it deals with a specific period — the war years and through into the 50s so that between them, they record sides of village life over three decades. The story is however not yet complete . . .

During the whole period covered by this book, the countryside was changing and the lifestyle of the village blacksmith was changing too. Whether by design or by accident I cannot be too sure, but farming, which had been my Mother's main interest, was taking precedence in my life over the blacksmith's craft my Father taught me.

The role of the blacksmith as farrier, shoeing the heavy shires and workhorses that were the prime suppliers of motive power in the countryside had almost become redundant, as tractors took over, yet there was more work for the smith, a new type of skilled work, repairing the implements drawn behind the tractors, and putting right the damage caused by eager farmers' sons with their newly bought welders. For they had not yet acquired sufficient skill and experience to be able to use their new machines to full advantage.

We did not know it at the time, but we were living at the crossroads of change when the old traditional crafts of the countryside were being replaced by a faster more modern technology. In its own way, the countryside absorbed this new age of technology, and somehow as I hope to record in a third book placed on it its own stamp.

Just as this book has recorded how a rural community embraced and came to terms at its leisure with an age of comparative slow change so in the next, I hope to show how, as blacksmith became farmer, Shropshire was also changing faster than we realised. Yet curiously its people did not alter in character or outlook nor in their sense of humour.

Both my books have introduced readers to the people who put colour and fun and humour into my life. In a curious way our stories cannot be separated: they are as much a part of my life as I am of theirs.

Brow Farm, Frankton.   ALF STRANGE
August 1986.

Chapter 1

'The Invasion Before It Began'

WAR with Germany was just starting, or to be more precise, was just about to start when our little village was invaded by evacuees from Liverpool. They were mainly Catholic, (without trying to be 'uppish' at all, — from Scotland Road, Liverpool, in the main) a different religion from us humble country folk. Furthermore, they were 'townies', used to electricity, running water, flush toilets, the lot as far as we Frankton-ites went. What a shock it must have been to them to have to go to bed by candlelight.

Fights soon broke out between them and us country kids, but only with fists those days. 'Putting the boot in' was unheard of. However, I think things soon started to settle down. They took over the Parish Hall for their school room and I remember their Headmaster's name was Mr. Merriot (nicknamed Merry Legs) and the Father's name was Father Horan (nicknamed Daddy Horan).

At 8 o'clock on the Saturday morning, the apple tree in the garden next to where my school mate Tom Speke lived, was loaded with apples — I saw them myself. (I might well have nipped in to help myself to a couple, but I knew they were not ready for eating, and had been caught out before). Come 8 o'clock that night, there was not a blinking apple on the tree. (A hurricane? Well, I suppose you could call it something like that. But the only wind that had anything to do with it was that kind of wind which goes with eating urder-ripe apples, — belly ache wind. For the Saturday in question was none other than the 2nd September, 1939. Those on pension *will* remember that Saturday. The hurricane all had two legs and two hands each, but only one mouth and one receptacle tummy. Most of those children had never seen an apple attached to a tree before; some had never seen an apple. So what could you expect? They just ran riot as soon as the first one spotted them, — not just that tree in the Perthy lane, but all over Frankton.

Afer stripping the tree, they wandered down slowly to the Smithy. Dad happened to be shoeing a bargee's cart horse. One lad came screaming back up the lane, shouting in broad Scouse, — 'Eh, — there's a bloke down 'ere in a shed what's setting fire to a 'orse.'

The Billetting Officer in charge of fixing up the evacuees arrived at a fairly big house, enquiring of the aged couple, as to how many rooms they had. He was pleased to hear that they had six spare bedrooms. 'Right,' he said, 'Twelve evacuee children for you when the time comes,' and away he went. A week went by when the Billetting Officer received a 'phone call from the old gentleman, informing him that his wife had passed away, and that it would be very difficult for him to cope with the 12 children. Back went the Billeting Officer, and he said to the old boy, 'Look, the choice is yours, you either have twelve children or six expectant mothers.' Quick as a flash the old boy replied: 'I will have the six expectant mothers as long as they don't expect too much.'

The evacuees throughout the country came from every large populated area, Manchester, London, Birmingham, Newcastle, etc. Only Shropshire and Denbighshire had Liverpool children, and maybe only Ellesmere and district, from Scotland Road.

The kids arrived with their pinned cardboard labels, and their gas masks, some crying for their parents. Others couldn't care less, and were in trouble before the night was out. Some wetted the bed, — but who could blame them — not me.

A few mothers arrived, but were back on the train by Tuesday, because we did not sport a pub. Many of the children went back before Christmas 1939. Those old enough, will remember that for the first five months or so it was a 'phoney war', with the likelihood of peace 'breaking out' anytime. Some stayed on. At least two stayed and married local lads, and are in the area still.

Before the mothers went back, they came to us lads on that hot September day. We had the last jar of Mother's home brewed beer. The women offered us whatever money we cared to ask for the jar. We didn't sell. We daren't, — not the last one!

One of the lads, — a well behaved boy and a favourite with the village people, stayed on longer than most. In later life he went in for the Roman Catholic Church. He is a Priest in a special calling. He has been to see us twice in recent years — well I say 'recent' and our Valerie is now thirty-two, I link his first visit with her, because he called quite unexpectedly, on her Christening Day.

The second time was more conspicuous, he arrived in a mini-bus or maybe it was a proper bus, with a group of Roman Catholic Clergymen, Priests, Fathers, the lot. He wanted them to see Hardwick Pool, and 'his' War-Time Village. Vera, my wife, coped, as she always does.

That reminds me of a cousin of mine who was a driving instructor in the Police. He used to bring a bus load of young policemen, quite often, stopping at Ellesmere for Hayward's pork pies and coming up to the Perthy for a cup of tea to go with their pies. One day I was in the Smithy, when all this lot trooped out of the bus and into the Smithy — all in uniform. There were three or four lads watching me work, (I was seldom without spectators when school was not in session). As the policemen filled the wide doorway, I dropped my hammer, and started to take my apron off, saying as I did, 'Alright Officers, I'll come quietly.' The look on the lads faces was worth seeing, one blurted out, 'Why? What 'ave you done, Alf?' Another was even more 'patriotic', — 'Do you want us to come with ya, Alf, to deny it?'

I'm rambling again.

The children from Liverpool were most interested in our 'Paraffin Man.' They had not seen anything like that before.

Jack Allen from Ellesmere had a round selling paraffin, (candles, matches, soaps and all kinds of hardware), since before the 1914-18 War. I remember him coming round with a pony and cart. He had called at our house ever since my Dad got married. Later, he used a little lorry with all his little bits and pieces on the side and two large paraffin tanks, one on either side. His son, Fred, who was a bit older than me, used to come with him up to the time of his going into the Air Force.

Fred was in the Ellesmere Boy Scouts, and many times we Frankton lads played football on their field at the back of what used to be the Wallasey home, against Ellesmere Scouts. The Wallasey home was used to give poor children from Liverpool and surrounding areas a country holiday, (before that it had been a Private School for girls, known as the 'Ladies' College'). After the war it became a private house. Now, alas, it has been demolished and in its place have been built some homes for Senior Citizens.

The first time I remember Fred coming with his dad to our house, he was in his early teens, — before the war. Jack, his Dad said to him, 'Watch Joe Strange in case he pinches anything off the lorry.' That particular day Jack had a bright red bristle broom on the far side of the lorry, away from the house. Jack went into the house for his customary cup of tea, Dad browsing around the lorry, and Fred watching his every movement like a hound. My Dad, knowing that the matches were on the other side of the lorry, said to Fred: 'Box of matches Fred, please.' Fred goes round the other side of the lorry, as quick as a flash my Dad picked up the bright red broom and threw it over the hedge into our field.

A moment later Jack came out of the house and my Dad said: 'Jack, have you got one of those bright red brooms on?' Jack said to Fred: 'Go and get it from the other side of the lorry.' Panic stations! Fred could not find the broom. 'It was there when I went into the house,' said Jack, 'are you sure you kept your eye on Joe, Fred?' 'Never let him out of me sight,' said Fred. On that my Dad said: 'What's that in the field, Fred?' Jack told Fred: 'I told you to keep your eye on him,' and he said to my Dad, 'Blast you Joe, and your country tricks.' Fred never ever bothered again to keep his eye on my Dad. Just another bit of country wit and leg pulling.

Jack Allen came one morning with a black eye. 'Been fighting, Jack?' said my Dad. 'I anna,' replied Jack. 'Never again will I interfere in a husband and wife quarrel, Joe.' It seems Jack had knocked on the door of one of his customers, with a terrible commotion going on inside. Opening the door, the sight that confronted him was the husband holding his wife by the throat. Jack said he was sure she was going to be choked to death. He said: 'I dived in and managed to

12

free her, and knocked her husband to the ground. Turning around to see if the wife was alright. *She* hit me with the broom blacking my eye shouting: 'You leave my husband alone, you bully'.'

All through the War Jack Allen came every week to keep the business together for Fred to come back to. But sadly Fred passed away only a few years after his father. Will the likes of them ever return? I doubt it. Fred, and his Dad before him, used to keep his hardware, paraffin and soaps etc., in a little red and black shed, in a field at the back of Cambrian Avenue in Ellesmere, the field is now a housing estate. It had been 'the paraffin field' for such a long time.

I remember Jack Allen would reckon up Dad's bill on the wrapping paper of the match boxes; and I also remember he gave Vera and me a wedding present, — a wicker shopping basket, which we still have.

Getting back to the evacuees, we had some very special ones. They didn't all hail from Scotland Road. Hardwick Hall, which at one time had as many as a dozen servants, was not being lived in at the start of the war. It was commandeered for blind children from a school in Manchester, — Henshaws Institution for the Blind. I think about fifty or sixty blind children were evacuated there for the duration, complete with teachers and helpers, etc. What a contrast to what it had been! They blended well into village life and one got to know the teachers. One teacher I particularly remember was the Music teacher, Mr. Dudley. He himself was totally blind, but in no time at all, he knew his way around our village. What a wonderful organist he was and he gave recitals in Frankton Church.

We village lads were invited down to play with the blind lads from the Hall and I think from then, I came to appreciate the blessing of good sight. They played football by sound, listening to where the ball bounced, or to the teachers' voices shouting to them which way to run. Today I smile when I read of the wages players receive for doing something they like, but I am sure that they could not have got more enjoyment out of a game of football than those lads did on Hardwick Park. Football hooligansim, the wrecking of trains, crowds running riot terrifying young and old, seemed a far cry from the football that those lads played. I wonder where we have gone wrong?

I started the chapter by calling it 'The Invasion Before It Began'. These last paragraphs I think had better be: 'The Invasion After It

Was All Over.' I include them to give you an insight into our village of Welsh Frankton.

Hardwick Hall was Col. John Kynaston's residence in peace-time, a Tory, little different from thousands of other landed gentry up and down the country. He owned the Perthy and expected his tenants there and of his farms at Hordley to sport blue rosettes.

One event that sticks in my mind is the Election of 1945. All the teachers of the blind children must have been strong Labour supporters, because on Hardwick Back Gates, Labour posters began to appear. I shudder to think what might have happened had they done it before the war. Bright green posters canvassing for the Labour party! It was as bad as shouting 'Enoch Powell' in Birmingham or 'Maggie Thatcher' in the Rhondda.

The blind boys and their teachers remained with us to the end of the war, — and until the August 1945 Election.

Chapter 2

' The Last Days at The School on The Hill '

BEFORE I get to the 'body' of my stories just at the start of the war I must mention a few more stories of my pre-war school days. It may be remembered from the first book, my elementary village school was at the top of the Brow, it wasn't Harrow!

One story concerns Albert Ankers, — the father of the girl who used to drink the milk and top up the can from the well. He had been wounded very badly in the 1914-18 war, and his job was to deliver the daily papers. He had many children and one day he came to Frankton school to see the Head teacher because she had caned one of them. She was a relief teacher, who came after Mr. Clayton Jones left in 1938 to go to Criftins as Head. We, at Frankton school had temporary relief teachers for a month or so at a time, until a permanent Head was appointed.

The relief had caned one of the Ankers children and Albert went to school next morning to ask why. He knocked the school door. The teacher opened it and enquired who he was and what he wanted. He told her and was invited in. There was no private room or office to take him only a space at the top of the classroom.

She proceeded to give him a lecture on how she intended to re-organise Frankton school and tighten up on discipline. If she wanted to cane his children, or in fact, any children, she was quite within her rights to do so.

We were all amazed at the dressing down she was giving poor Albert as we sat at our desks, arms folded. He had taken his cap off and was quite humble with her. He was 'yes, Miss', 'no, Miss', 'see it doesn't happen again, Miss', and this seemed to make her even more aggressive.

She was obviously self-assured and addressed the rest of us to the effect that the same thing would befall us if we stepped out of line. Little was she to know that she was about to encounter humiliation.

She turned to Albert and dismissed him as if he were one of her pupils, telling him to go and not come 'meithering' her again on her capabilities as a teacher. She turned away with a smug smile on her face. He turned to go and as he reached the door, his hand on the latch, he turned, looking at the teacher, and said in a loud voice: 'Missus'. 'Yes?', she shouted back. 'Yo wanna think yourself lucky. It's a good job my missus dinna come, 'er'd a 'screwed your bloody neck!'

On that note, he left. We roared with laughter. Albert, in one sentence had summed up the situation in a nut-shell, and he hit the nail on the head better than any blacksmith could have done. I can see the teacher's face now, — like a beetroot. She was speechless, and do you know that from that day on she seemed to mellow towards us kids. She left soon afterwards and I often wonder what the outcome would have been if Jane Ankers had come instead of Albert, because knowing Mrs. Ankers she *would* have 'screwed her bloody neck'.

Every Shrove Tuesday (Pancake Day), Frankton Top Class used to have a paper-chase. Weeks before, old exercise books and old papers would be torn up into small squares, enough to fill a couple of satchels. Two of the best runners would be selected to act as hares and given ten minutes' start. The rest of the school would then be let loose to follow the paper trail around the village and across the fields, in all about five miles. Very few had running pumps, mainly hob-nailed boots or clogs, but it didn't seem to matter. To be allowed out of school for an hour or two was a real treat. Simple things maybe, but quite a day in our young lives. I sometimes wonder now if there had been coaching and contracts, Frankton school might have supplied an Olympic runner, who knows? But I thank Clayton Jones for letting us have a paper-chase on Pancake Day. As it comes round every year, I turn my mind back to those paper-chases of school days. It doesn't seem to be as long from one Pancake Day to the next now as it used to be — I wonder if it has something to do with age! The last one I was priviliged to take part in was 1939's Shrove Tuesday, — before the 3rd September of that historic year, — but I make no excuse for including the account here.

Quite apart from the Shrove Tuesday paper-chase, the different seasons would bring out different games. Conkers would be contested when they were ready, — early Autumn. Someone would have a forty-niner'. All sorts of methods would be tried to get a better conker than your schoolmate. Baking them in the oven or boiling them in water, and one trick we had was to have half an iron nut on one end of our string and a conker on the other; holding the nut in your hand until it was your smack! There weren't many conkers that could withstand a smack with a $\frac{1}{2}''$ iron nut. Of course, if you had 'strings', you were caught out; ('Strings' was when the strings wound around each one.) The best thing for boring a hole through a conker would be a horse-nail, and many is the horse-nail I have pinched out of me Dad's shoeing box for other kids to bore a hole in their conker.

Marbles was another game played every Spring! There were two forms at least. In the playground we made a ring of the clay marbles, with one in the middle. The aim was to hit the middle one with a flip of the thumb. Sometimes there would be a small circle of marbles in the centre of the other ring; or even a glass alley.

Pride of our Alleys, — didn't mean what Gracie Fields sang about. A glass alley was bigger than the clay marble, some twice as big, some *four* times as big, — with beautiful coloured strips of dyed cotton thread inside.

You could get 20 marbles for a penny, but some of the exquisite alleys would cost as much as that each. So it was only the capitalists, — or was it the bullies, — that managed more than two or three of those? The other marble game was played in the gutter going home from school. (I rarely had time to take part).

When marbles were getting tiring, — the alleys would come in handy for swopping for a top and whip. One alley for a top, — we soon made a whip from a leather boot lace. Top and whip was a Summer game. Halfpenny Jack Jumpers from the Top Shop and a

17

piece of string and a bit of wood to make the whip with, if you wanted to do it proper like.

Bowler and hook! That was a great thing. A bowler race around the Perthy was something. Dad used to make them for about a penny, or if you did so much work, he would make you one for nothing. I think in 1987 we will have a sponsored bowler race around Ellesmere for the Cottage Hospital if I can find enough 'owd uns' to run.

Sometimes, if we lost our 'football' (a third hand tennis ball, probably found by the tennis courts in Ellesmere) in the ditch on the other side of the school wall, or our 'cricket bat' had been split with no substitute yet forth-coming, we would be relegated to playing tick. If the girls had no ball either, they would join in with us. If the one ticked was big enough she would have to give a kiss instead of taking on as hunter. It was noticeable that some of the girls didn't seem to run as quickly as when they were playing rounders! That reminds me of the two young ladies walking through Cremorne Gardens, the one said to the other, 'Mabel, I believe we're being followed; don't walk so fast.'

Although I was never very good at school lessons, when I look back at that time I agree they were the happiest days.

Recalling schooldays the other day with Ron Jones, sitting in his office in the playground by the old school which he has turned into a trailer works and repair business, we started to talk of the characters who have been to Frankton school and the characters who used to go past while we were there, before and during the war.

Cattle being driven by road to Oswestry market to be sold; ponies and traps; people on bikes; and I once saw some elephants going from a circus in Oswestry to Ellesmere, also bears, some coloured ponies all following one another. I remember Jack Reeves taking a pig to Oswestry with a piece of rope tied around one back leg to stop him getting away. R.S.P.C.A. was unheard of or, if they were, the war effort came first.

We talked about a big fir tree that still stands in John Lewis's field. It must be 100 feet high. We used to climb it in our dinnertime and eat jam 'butties' in the highest branches. It is a wonder some of us did not break our necks.

Also, we recalled sitting on the roof of an old shed not far from the school, when one day Constable Heatley from Whittington caught a gang of us up there. He took our names in his black book. We thought that we were going to be 'put inside' for a fair stretch. I can see him now, and he warned us of our future conduct and said that we would be hearing from him or the court in due course. 46 years later, we are still waiting to hear, but at the time, we were scared stiff.

It only seems like yesterday, and we both agreed that life really is short but who was it who said: 'It is not how long you live, but how you live,' that is the test. We talked of the families that lived a long way from school. Kids from Lower Berghill, Jessie Rogers from Hardwick. She had irons on both legs having had polio when three years old but still had to walk a mile and a half up our fields and along the main road. Very often she would break the irons and be helpless until my father repaired them in the smithy. Hospital cars, taxis, buses to bring you to school, what were they?

Only today I heard of a firm wanting an apprentice workman but because the bus service did not run at the right hours, how was a 16-year-old going to get from Oswestry to St. Martins — a distance of about four miles? There were no applicants for the job. Are bikes so out of date?

Nicholas's children and the ones from Dutton's from Old Martin used to walk about 2½ miles across fields and how we envied them when Clayton Jones, the Headmaster, let them out of school a quarter of an hour early. How I used to wish he would let me go to save those dreaded speed tests he used to put up on the blackboard for the last ten minutes of our school day. Mrs. Walter Jones, Mrs. Colesby and Mrs. Hayward of Bottle Row (houses opposite the school), would for a halfpenny make a cup of cocoa for some of the children. 2½d a week — what price a cup of coffee today? In a motor-cafe 28p at least. 5/6d in the old money!

Before going on I would like to recap a little more on schooldays. Only an old dirt-ridden playground we had for football and cricket, the same for the girls to play rounders. No staying in at playtime, out we went in all weathers. The central heating was just a big old coal or log fire.

School books used to come about every six months to Frankton Station. That was a good time when you got older to go to fetch them with a four-wheeler truck borrowed from Brow Farm, — their milk truck it was. You could stretch out fetching the books from the

19

Station to a whole day if the school boss was in a good mood. Exercise books, ink that went into ink wells, pens with nibs, (no biros, no calculators), now it's computers!

The last twelve months at Frankton school for me consisted mainly of digging the head teacher's (Mrs. Ramsey) garden, and building up the wall between the field and the playground. I think she realised that I was never meant to be Prime Minister or Chancellor of the Exchequer. It was easier all round to let me do more or less what I wanted. It saved her some sleepless nights.

I once managed to waste half-a-day tending about two roots of rhubarb in her garden, telling her how difficult it was to grow, as it had to be covered up with straw, or old buckets with holes in. One day I remember we had a new ball in the stock and I threw it across the class-room and it gave her a clack on the ear, that cost me three or four suspended playtimes. I would sooner have had the cane. As I look back at my schooldays I recall my teachers' names — Clayton Jones, Mrs. Jeffrey, Miss Kent (now Mrs. Forrester), Miss Bolton who took me to hospital when I swallowed a drawing pin, Miss Williams, and Miss Griffiths, both from Oswestry. I wonder if they would believe their useless pupil would one day write a book. The odds they would have got with a 'bookie' would have been fantastic.

Only a 'few' years ago, or so it seems, during the Suez Crisis of 1956, petrol was rationed, and I let Miss Griffiths have a 5-gallon petrol coupon, and I reminded her then that she had always taught me to be honest and not to do anything wrong, and she told me to forget about that, just for that day!

I say 'Thank You' to all of them. They did their best with a completely hopeless case. They did, at least, teach me right from wrong, and one accepted any puishment that they handed out if one had done anything wrong. There was no going home crying to mother, because you would get another clack to go with it. Other lads used to say that if they went home from our smithy saying that Joe Strange had kicked their arse, there would be another kick to go with that too.

As I look back over my life, I think one of the worse things officialdom did was to allow village schools to close. I think that children up to the age of ten or eleven need to be brought up in their own environment. Do we need central heated classrooms to make us

20

better people? If you've got what it takes, you will make your way in the world.

I think we are trying to educate kids who, I am sure, if allowed to make up their own minds, would prefer to leave school earlier. If you want your son or daughter to learn a trade, speaking from experience, I would sooner have a lad at 14 so I could teach him my ways. After he has been at school until he is 17, he knows more, or thinks he does, than his boss, just as I did. Yo dunna need a rucka' O' levels or A' levels to be a first-class tradesman. Common sense! I quote out of an old blacksmithing book, the requirements of a farrier, I think that it sums up all I have said:

> *A Blacksmith.* A good common school education is necessary. More will do no harm. Further requisites are — a healthy body. Not too tall. A liking for work. Aptness and an active mind. Fearlessness, dexterity, a good eye for proportion. (I presume that meant a horse?) And finally, careful selection of a master instructor.

> A *farrier shoes horses,* a *blacksmith works with iron.* We were taught both trades in my apprenticeship.

Early in the war, shooting was still allowed on the estates in the Ellesmere area, and the bigger lads were chosen to go 'beating' all around the Hardwick Estate, at Hordley, and the Woodhouse Estate at Rednal. The keepers at Rednal Estate were Ben and Tom Tomkins. Woodhouse Estate belonged to a squire called Mostyn Owen. We used to go 'beating' on a Saturday for 3/6d a day, but we also had a good dinner. Men used to act as loaders for the gentry, so that they always had a spare gun loaded. This particular story is about one old boy who had about forty shots but not one bird. He said to his loader: 'What do you think I am doing wrong?' 'You are missing the birds!' said the loader. 'I know that, you ruddy fool!' came the reply. After the day's shoot, this particular gentleman had not shot a bird and his loader was heard to say that he thought the birds had more chance of being struck by lightning than of being shot by his boss!

In the old days, birds were reared in their natural state out in the wilds, and I have come across many a pheasant's nest in a hedgerow around the farm, with the hen pheasant sitting on her eggs. You could walk within a few feet of her and not see her, so naturally would

21

she blend with her surroundings. Now, a new breed of shooter has arrived. Birds are reared in thousands for the pleasure of our so-called affluent society, when I believe a day's shooting can cost well in excess of £100.

Like country sports, inflation does not stand still, and one must remember that without them, thousands more could be out of work. If one wants to ride to the hounds, shoot game, fish, etc., one must be prepared to pay, and as I have always said: 'If you can't spend your money as you wish, it will be a sorry day for this little island of ours.'

At the start of the war, before I left school, Nobby Jones of No. 9 Lower Perthy had ferrets for sale. We lads at the blacksmith's shop managed to persuade Mother to buy us one off him. He brought two in a sack for us to choose. Putting his hand in the sack to grab one around the neck, the other one bit his thumb, and as Nobby pulled his hand out of the sack one ferret was hanging on to his thumb. He looked at my Mother with with the ferret still hanging on and said: 'I wunna have this one because the bugger canna half bite, missus.'

As we were coming home from school one Wednesday a cattle lorry passed us on the Brow. A farmer or cattle dealer, sitting in front with the driver leaned out of the passenger doorwindow, heaving his heart out, — too much beer at the Cambrian (better known as the 'Pub on catch 'em Corner') I suppose. Further down on the side of the road was a top and bottom pair of false teeth.

We lads looked at them and Brian Jones kicked them into the ditch, and we went on our way home, thinking no more about them. After we had done our jobs at home and had our tea, I remembered and told Mother about the false teeth we had seen on the roadside. 'You go and fetch them straight away,' said Mother. Both Frank and I were loath to do that. 'Get you off,' said my Mother in that tone of voice we knew there was no point arguing against. 'Here,' she said, 'Put them in this 2 lb. sugar bag.' A dark blue bag it was, one of Pat King's special bags that she used to weigh out the loose sugar in. We found the teeth, but neither of us could pick them up with our hands, so Frank held the bag open and I manouvred the teeth into it with me foot.

Mother tipped them out when we got home into a bucket of water, rinsed them under the pump, and dried them off with an old piece of cloth, and put them up on the top of the old cupboard in the back-kitchen.

A week or so later in the *Oswestry Advertiser* a £2 reward was offered to the finder of a set of false teeth lost on the Welsh Frankton-Oswestry Road. I expect the money came in handy to buy clothes or shoes for us lads.

One of the last achievements I managed before leaving school was to swallow a drawing pin! I was putting up some paper on the school wall with drawing pins. I had them in my mouth. I don't really know what happened, but I somehow managed to swallow one. Miss Bolton was the relief teacher at the time, and I told her. She had to get Miss Williams, who was teaching the middle class, to look after the top class as well, while she ran me to the Doctor in Elles-mere in her little Austin Ruby Saloon.

The Doctor asked whether it stuck in my throat, I said I could not feel it anywhere. 'Right', he said 'Go home and get your Mother to make you some cotton wool butties and with luck nature will take its course.' Forty-six years later I presume that must have happened and my only lasting memories of that day now, is that I had a ride in a car, and was allowed a day off school. I was probably lucky not to have had the cane for attempting to steal school property! Because the cane and I had close associations.

In December 1939 I came through Frankton School gates for the last time as a pupil. Arriving home, the first words my father said were, 'Well lad, your playing days are over.' I was at the ripe old age of fourteen; but they weren't really.

The other day I came across two original invoices (what they were doing in my possession I dunna know), for day-trips in 1921 and 1922 respectively.

Cost of boat trip to Pant — Sunday School Trip, 1921:
(Before my time, our Tom would be on it before he got 'expelled' to Ellesmere)

Hire of Boat	....	£1 10	0
Locks	....	12	6
Teas for 60	....	£5 7	6
60 Oranges	....	8	9
60 Buns	....	8	9
Nuts	....	2	10
TOTAL COST	....	£8 10	4

Trip to New Brighton, June 1922:

(Tom would be in Ellesmere now but Bill would be on it)

Hire of 3 Char-a-bancs	£7	10	0
Teas for 41 @ 1/- each	£2	1	0
Lunch for 3 drivers		4	0
3 waitress tips		5	0
TOTAL COST FOR DAY TRIP ...	£10	0	0

Again proving the point that inflation had been with us for quite a long time. In fact we 'boast' of 5 Woodbines for 2d, but before 1914 they were 5 for 1d.

Chapter 3

' All for a Shilling a Day '

JOHN HAYWARD was the first village lad to be called up to the army, soon to be followed by Raymond Jones. Next was my brother Bill. Things were getting desperate! He received his letter 'OHMS' on 7th January 1940. In it was his calling up papers telling him to report a week later 15th January to Catterick Camp. Was it really 43 years ago? Emily and Joe Strange's son off to the Army! I can see them still, standing on the old Smithy Bank watching Bill go down our field to catch the train at Frankton Station, tears in their eyes.

The break-up of their family was beginning. Tom, who was working at Chester, was still coming home at week-ends. We did not see a lot of him. He was courting a local girl, Elsie Cook from Cae Goody Farm, Cae Goody Lane. They were married on 13th May 1940 at Ellesmere Church. Bill was to be best man but could not get leave from the Army. If my Mother could have given the Powers-that-be who would not allow that the length of her tongue, they would have been glad to have given Bill leave to get rid of her, but it was not to be. Sam Hayward of the Post Office, one of Tom's pals, stood in for Bill at the wedding. I remember it so well, because I had my first pair of long trousers. The wedding breakfast was at the Black Lion, Ellesmere.

Tom was the next to be called up on 12th December 1940, and

25

Jack was next. Three of the sons now gone, one in the Artillery, one in the Signal Corps, and one in the Royal Army Service Corps. Letters would arrive home from them with reasonable regularity and that was my mother's job to open them and read them out to my Dad and me at breakfast time. If a week went by without a letter, my mother would get a bit naggy and Norman Peake, our regular postman would get the blame. I remember him saying to my mother one morning: 'Yum a miserable 'oud devil Em. It inna my fault there is no letters'.

Although only Frank and I were still at home, money was still short in our house as farming and blacksmithing were still in a fairly depressed state. However, we in the country were still very fortunate though, as rationing had not really started to affect us by then. It was to, later on as the war progressed. It was quite surprising how, when one of my brothers came home on leave, extra egg and bacon appeared as if by magic, and the tin of peaches that we other two sons had not seen for months, came to the table. I used to think that it was like the Bible story of the return of the Prodigal Son. All too soon the 48-hour pass would be up and the bike ride to Gobowen Station would be on again. Many is the time during the early part of the war I used to ride one bike and push the other to meet one of them off the train.

The war in Europe in the early days seemed so far away, when suddenly it all seemed to happen with the fall of France and one realised there was only 22 miles of water between us and the German Army. German bombers used to fly over our little village on their way to bomb Birkenhead or Liverpool. Little did we realise how lucky we were to be living in the country, although two bombs fell quite close — one by Hardwick Back Drive Gate, and the other along by Halston. By now though, Frankton Home Guard had been formed, but that's another story.

The war in Europe seemed to be quite stationary at that time, apart from the regular night time raids on our bigger towns. There seemed to be more action in the middle East. Then came the first news that shook our little village community and stunned everyone. Raymond Jones of Brow Farm had been killed in Tobruk. A real gloom seemed to settle for weeks over the villagers and it surely brought the realisation home to us of the cruelty of war. Everyone's thoughts and prayers turned to his family. The first Frankton lad to die in the 1939 war on a foreign field. I was about sixteen at the time and my memories of Raymond were how good he was at football. He had had trials with Everton before he was called up. Then my memories would swing back to the games we had played together on the fields of Frankton. Football on Hardwick Park, cricket on our big field. He was a true village lad, full of life and energy.

Barely twenty-one he was. A year or so later, another lad — Geoff James went missing in an aircraft raid over Germany, 'believed killed'. Another school pal and friend killed, cut down in his youth. As one gazed at the War Memorial outside the church and saw all the names of previous village lads who had died a bare 20 years earlier in the 1914-18 war, one had more to shudder about. That was a war that was supposed to end all wars. It was looking at those names that brought home to me the tragic loss and grief that older villagers had been through before. Life must go on, and maybe mankind will learn to live in peace with one another, at some future date.

The lads in khaki and their 'I'll walk beside you' forage caps, used to march from Park Hall, depending on the Sarge, mostly singing:

'All for a shilling a day, breakfast and nothing to pay,'
'You've had your breakfast in bed before, you'll not get it there anymore
'All for a shilling a day, learning the words that a sergeant — can say,'
'All for a shilling a day.'

— And —

'Bless 'em all, Bless 'em all,'
'The long and the short and the tall,'
'Bless all the Sergeants and W.O. Ones,'
'Bless all the Corporals and their b - - - - - - - sons.'

— And of course —
— the one that boomeranged on us —

'We're going to hang out our washing on the Siegfried line,'
'If the Siegfried line's still there.'

27

'Run rabbit, run rabbit, run, run, run,'
'Don't let the farmer have his fun, fun, fun,'
'He'll get by without his rabbit pie,
'So run rabbit, run rabbit, run, run, run.'

Later, we in the T.A. used to sing them, up-dated versions in some instances and songs like, 'There'll Always Be An England'.

Early in the War, I remember my brother Jack, home on leave, shot a wild goose flying over our field. Jack Haynes was with us. Unfortunately, it fell into Hardwick Pool, and the problem was how to get the goose out of the pool and into the pot. The boat was padlocked into the Boathouse. Then, Jack Haynes had a brainwave. He suggested we went went back up to the smithy and get Miss Kenyon's pig cooler that had been brought to have some hoops put on it, to make it water-tight. A pig cooler is shaped like an oblong boat. It is the pig cooler in which you salt the pig after it has been killed. Well, up we lads came, got the pig cooler, carried it and rolled it to the waters edge. By this time, the goose had floated further out into the middle of the pool. Who was to go out into the water on the pig cooler-cum-boat? Jack Haynes, not mincing words said: 'You are the lightest, so you go!' (I've left some of the mincemeat out). I knew that it would be pointless to argue. The decision had been taken. We pushed the cooler-cum-boat out into the water, and to our dismay, the water started to leak in. 'I inna goin' out in that,' I said to them both. Haynes then found an old salmon tin. 'Here, take this with you, you can bale out the water with one hand while you paddle with the other.'

Very apprehensively, this I started to do, getting out into the middle of the pool with the water well over my ankles and rising. I managed to grab the dead goose and haul it into the boat (cooler). The extra weight made it sink a bit lower into the water and the journey back seemed like an eternity and I was glad to hear the bottom of the cooler scrape the bank. The whole operation had taken about an hour. The reason that the cooler had leaked was because it had been left out in the sun. If it had been put into water the rims would have tightened up and would have sealed up the cracks in the cooler. The goose was a tasty meal for our family for a few days. We never told me Mother and Dad how we had recovered it! Their reaction would probably have been, what if the cooler had sunk in about 15 feet of water, who would have got it out then and what would Miss Kenyon have said? Never mind poor little Alf!

The remarkable sequel to this story is that the other day I had a letter from a farmer's wife about my first book, and she mentions in her letter that she was the girl who brought the pig cooler to our shop in a pony and trap and recalls it nearly slipped off the cart at Brynore Bank when she was bringing it in to be repaired . . . She also recalls how she delivered milk to Frankton School with a wild little pony called Betsy, and that when the army lorries went past them, — with their canvas tops flapping — she and the other girl had to hang on, one to each rein, and pull like hell to hold the pony. So ends the story of Miss Kenyon who lived at Brynore Hall and her pig cooler. The girl, Joy Strain, was later to marry a German prisoner of war, who worked on a nearby farm. His name was Fritz Hormann. They now farm very successfully in mid-Wales. Now, 43 years later, they will know what happened to the pig cooler she brought up to the Smithy.

I wonder if either of us could have forseen the future. Perhaps it was as well we did not. What a calamity it would have been if the cooler had fallen off the cart, or worse still, sunk in Hardwick Pool. It would have been village news for days in spite of the National News. It is almost as good a story as the *Yellow Rolls Royce* film.

One night at Randel Jones, the Mount Farm, at Elson, we members of the Ellesmere Young Farmers were given a talk by a Ministry Official, an overweight woman in breeches and long stockings. In single hen cages were hens of various breeds, and she was telling us youngsters the good and bad points of the different breeds. In one cage was an old Sussex hen which had seen many summers (and winters, come to that). After examining the hen for about a minute the remarks she made was: 'This hen is only fit for eating, a real old boiler. It's a waste of good corn to keep her. If she were mine I would wring her neck.' As the Ministry Instructress lady moved further up the yard. Randel Jones, the farmer's son, produced a hen egg, slipped it into the old hen's cage and made a cackling noise with his mouth. The look of amazement on her face is hard to describe. And do you know, I dunna think her was very amused either!

Chapter 4

' A Job with a Pension — Almost '

SOON after leaving school to work at home, I wrote after many jobs but with no luck. Work was hard to come by. I tried for a job at the Railway Depot at Oswestry. No luck! A butcher's job at the Co-Op in Ellesmere — missed out again. Joe Butler did offer me a temporary job in his bike shop in Ellesmere at 7/6d a week, Thursday afternoon and Sunday off. But I did not fancy life as a bike mender. Bad enough mending your own punctures, never mind other people's. Mother always used to be saying to me that her other three sons had got jobs with pensions when they retired. A very forward looking woman was my Mother, thinking about a job with a pension when you had only just left school at 14. She was thinking 50 years ahead.

My two elder brothers were in the Postal Service. Tom, the eldest, had started work as a telegraph lad in Ellesmere. Bill, the next, with six years between their ages, was a counter clerk at Oswestry Post Office. Jack, who had worked at Jos. Jones's blacksmith's shop at Alberbury for two years, had got a job on British Waterways as an apprentice blacksmith at Ellesmere under George Stokes. Harry Coleman, and Harry Horton from Lower Frankton were also in the blacksmith's shop at the Ellesmere Yard, making all the lock-gates for the canal from Northwich to Llangollen.

Emily Strange's three eldest had jobs with pensions. Three years difference in age between Bill and Jack, three years between Jack and me, and three years between my younger brother Frank and me. So after a six year gap between her two eldest sons, Emily planned her next for every three years. Perhaps it was a very good year for farming and blacksmithing. Every third year. The two are very much connected, as when agriculture is doing well the smith thrives. It is quite amazing the number of people who make a living out of the old dairy cow.

However, back to mine and my Mother's problem of 45 years ago. How to get her fourth son a job with a pension. Norman Peake the postman came with some secret news that they were 'wanting temporary staff at Ellesmere Post Office', and he would 'put a word in' for me. Was it not he who had got my other brothers their jobs in the Post Office? Norman promised that he would do his best. What more could one ask? Every day excitement was mounting. Then the letter arrived for me to go for interview with the Head Postmaster at Ellesmere. My clean white shirt, starched as only Mrs. Morgan could do it. Suit pressed, shoes cleaned until you could see your face in them and of course, the extra scrub around your ears and neck and away I went with my Mother's words ringing in my ears: 'take your cap off'; 'Stand up straight'; 'Speak when spoken to'. How was I going to remember all the instructions?

However, I must have got on alright until he asked how old I was. I told him I was fifteen. 'Oh dear you should be sixteen', replied the Postmaster. My spirits dropped. A failure again. I remember leaving his office close to tears. The ride home on my bike from Ellesmere to the Perthy seemed an eternity. Me Mother was as I expected, waiting for me by the door. 'No good', I said. 'I'm too young to be a postman.' 'Who said that?' 'I'll go and see 'im myself.' Emily's pride was dented. She was not having any Postmaster telling her that her son would not be good enough at 15 to be a temporary postman.

'Calm yourself down, Em' said my Dad, 'rule says you have got to be 16. Let it end there'. 'Aye, and rules was made to be broken. Wait till Norman Peake comes. I'll give 'im a piece of me mind', said she. Poor old Norman was going to get the blame. 'It inna Norman's fault', I said. 'He never thought about my age'. 'Well he should 'ave known, he calls here every day for a cup of tea, he should remember you being born'. 'Perhaps he does', I said, 'but you canna blame him'!

'Didn't you tell the Postmaster that Tom and Bill was working for the Post Office?' 'He already knew that', I said. Going upstairs to change out of my best clothes into my working ones, I thought 'Ah well, I am destined to be a blacksmith'. Norman the postman arrived with the afternoon delivery. Emily, as promised, gave him her views on the Post Office system. 'Dunna blame me, Em, I dunna make the rules' he said.

A week went by, my mother giving Norman the cold shoulder. She still thought that he could alter the system. Then it happened. Next day, Norman — all smiles — came with the news that Alf was to start at Ellesmere Post Office at 5.30 a.m. next Monday morning. What a different reception he had that day. Smiles all round and an extra cup of tea. I don't know how the rules were altered, or perhaps I was the only applicant for the job. I had to go on the Saturday morning to be given my post office bike. A big red one with a damn big carrier on the front. That was to be my machine for the next few weeks. Early to bed on the Sunday night with the usual scrub-up. Up the next morning about 4.30. My mother was already down and the fire was lit. An extra bit of bacon that morning for her fourth son Alf, starting a new *job with a pension* at the end of fifty-odd years.

Away I went, not having a clue as to what was expected of me, but I remember my mother saying, as it was wartime I would be delivering either happy or sad news to somebody's home, such was my mother's sensitivity. Arriving at the back door of the Post Office, it was already busy with activity with other postmen who had started earlier shifts. My round was to be the Dudleston Heath round. Alf Hewitt was the bloke in charge of the counter. I remember him. He was to help me sort out the letters for my round. I have never seen so much mail in all my life. What a job that was, getting the letters and parcels into separate bundles for the different areas of Dudleston Heath and Criftins. Letters were then numbered in order of delivery, parcels were strapped onto the carrier over the front wheel of the bike. All loaded up and ready to go, but wait a minute, — uniform, for a temporary postman consisted of an arm-band with the words *Post Office,* to wear on my arm only. At last I was away.

What a day! Start was at Elson Road in Ellesmere, up Cae Goody Lane as far as Bill Kynaston's. Turn round there, back along

Welsh Frankton School 1937

View from Chapel Door

the main road, Horseshoe Lane next, then up to Captain Owen's at Plas-yn-Grove, round the rest of Horseshoe Lane, out on to the main road by the Fox (the pub on the main road), up past the Working Men's Club, past Bob Jones, the Baker (affectionately known as Bob the Bun) then down past Criftins School out onto the road by the Vicarage, round to the Strains, Brynore Hall (a glass of milk there), onto the Balcarres, back then around Brynicochin. (Never knew there were so many different house names). Out again by Tom Steens, then down to Jack Powell's by Gravel Hole, turn around back for Arthon's Greenhill, turn left for Ellesmere, Davidsons, Edwards, Elson, Nicholls, Randel Jones, down the field to the old army dump (couple of cottages down there, Gwilym Jones lived in one), out on to the main road again at Osborne Corner, and then down the lane and over the railway line to the 'Dump', to Eddie Whitefield's, The Loop Farm. . . . . That was the last call, then back to the Post Office with letters I had collected out of the various letter boxes on my round. I left them at the Post Office then I headed for home at about 1 o'clock. Seven and a half hectic hours. I'd have my dinner then in would come my Dad, wanting a hand in the smithy until about 6 o'clock. I don't think he called a postman's job, work. This went on for about three weeks, then I was put onto the Hampton's Wood round.

Twenty two miles that was from start to fin' h. On that for a week and then the news I had been expecting. My life as a temporary postman was finished. The Postmaster, Mr. Poynton, said he would keep me in mind, but alas, that was it.

My job with a pension had come to an end, but it left me with a few happy memories. One was the day I got a puncture. I got it mended at Jack Peever's shop at Dudleston Heath. He charged me about 9d. I think I asked him for a bill to give to the Postmaster. This he did, but alas, when I presented it, the boss said that allowance was made in my wages for maintenance to my bike.

I once took the milk churn from Eddie Whitefield's gate, strapped it on to the carrier of me bike all the way down to his farm opening, about four gates across the railway line, only to be greeted by Mrs. Whitefield who demanded to know what I was doing with it. I told her that I had brought it down to save the boss going up in the pony and trap for it. I was told to take it back at once as it was left there to put the bread and meat in. I was only trying to help! and if she had known how I had struggled with the damn churn!!

My final story of my postman's career is about the Hampton Wood round. I always finished up at the Post Office in Welshampton at about 11.30. Some days you might get there for about ten past eleven, maybe wet through, but no! Mr. Jack Havers wouldn't open his Post box until 11.30, so you had to sit on the bench and wait, and many is the time that there would be no letters in the box after waiting.

As I sit here writing in my shed, it does not seem like 46 years ago since I had my job with pension attached. It was not to be, Emily and Joe Strange's fourth son was not destined to become Postmaster General. However, I would not have missed it for the world.

Chapter 5

'Entertaining Ourselves in the Blackout'

BLACKOUTS had to be fitted onto all windows. This included chapels and churches. Frankton Congregational Chapel, of which I am a member, decided that they would not go to that expense. In winter they would hold an afternoon service instead of an evening one. This my brother Frank and I agreed with. Chapel in the morning combined with Sunday School and Chapel in the afternoon. One less service for us to go in winter or so we worked it out. No such luck. The little Perthy Chapel decided they would put blackouts on their windows, and my mother said it would not do us any harm to go there in the evening. Three long services as well as Sunday School! The look on the preacher's face when he had preached at our Congregational Chapel in the afternoon and was using the same sermon at Perthy Chapel in the evening, and the two of us having heard him a couple of hours earlier was a 'bit much'. One night the preacher had not arrived at about seven o'clock, — half an hour late, — so Mr. Edwin Roberts said. 'We'll just have a hymn and a prayer and then we will go'. The hymn was 'Now the day is over'. We had come to the end, when in walked the preacher, nearly an hour late. He apologised and gave us an hour's sermon. At the end, he announced the hymn — his favourite, — none other than 'Now the day is over'.

I reckon that I must have been the most religious lad in the country, but I don't think it did me any harm, perhaps there are others who would say, 'nor good either'.

A youth club was formed in Frankton during the war. Every Tuesday night, we used to go up to the Parish Hall. There were about fifteen or twenty of us lads and girls all aged from about 14 to 16. We used to have all sorts of jobs to do. I remember Mr. Jeal was in charge of us lads and we would be taught wood carving by him. The girls would be knitting and making scarves and balaclava helmets for the soldiers. It was not all work though. We used to have gatherings, socials and dances with other youth clubs. Oswestry Youth Club used to meet at Woodside School. It was quite an event to go there and as I look back I remember the song we used to sing:

> Forty years on, when afar and asunder,
> Parted are those who are singing today,
> When we look back and regretfully wonder,
> What we were like in our work and our play.
>
> Then it may be there will often come on us,
> Glimpses of our youth like the catch of a song,
> Visions of our youth will float there before us,
> Echoes of dreamland will bear them along.
>
> Follow on, follow on,
> Till the days of our youth are o'er,
> And we meet here together no more.
> (Now the forty years have been and gone).

A gang of us from Frankton biked to Llangollen one Sunday for the day. We took jam butties with us. We hired a boat to go for a row up the canal and the inevitable happened — one of the girls fell in the canal. The poor lass was wearing a crepe dress, which when it started to dry out, shrank, revealing more than was intended. Frankton's first mini skirt ten years or more ahead of fashion. We always were a move ahead of everybody else.

Is it really 45 years ago? Quite a few of us are still left. Some have passed on and others are scattered over all parts of the world, but I expect that their minds, like mine, still wander back to their youth in Frankton, Oswestry and the surrounding villages.

Wouldn't it be nice if us that are left could have a good old get-together and reminisce, and I'll bet in many cases, instead of reminiscing, grandchildren would be the main topic of conversation.

Frankton had a Concert Party, Doris Brayne on the piano, Lily Jones's group singing to melodian accompaniment around an imitation camp fire; Jack Walsh singing as only he could. We had a couple of good sketches, — one called 'Farmhouse Teas'. Edna Miles, Margery her sister, Den Jones, Nesta Edwards, Lily Jones, Catherine Skinner and myself were in that, I remember. We toured the villages with our concert group — Tetchill, Hordley, Whittington, Criftins — raising money for various 'Welcome Home' funds, in spite of those slits for headlamp beams. The night we went to Hordley Parish Hall, we went in the back of Bill Howard's trailer with a bit of clean straw chucked over the floor boards. Talk about air conditioning, perfumed at that? Some of the modern pop groups would have wondered what had hit them. No need for after-shave, or use for it, after riding in the back of a cow trailer for a mile or two!

Mr. Strain of Brynore Hall formed a concert party and I was roped into that as well. What a terrific character he was! Full of devil, he liked a bit of fun. Glyn Baker, Frank Hockenell, Frank Evans, Amy Evans, — a few names that come to mind. Mrs. Clayton Jones was a wonderful soprano.

When Mr. Strain brought his concert party to Frankton, one item took the form of a quiz, a bit like *What's my Line*. Different members of the audience were briefed to ask certain questions and we on the panel would endeavour to answer and one of the questions my Dad asked was: 'How would the panel suggest the best way to court a country girl?' I know that my answer was, that I would have to ask my Dad because he courted my Mother who was a Tetchill lass. Frank Hockenell's reply was 'Treat um like a sick cow with a good hot bran mash with some treacle in to keep 'um warm.' Silly answers maybe, but they caused quite a bit of enjoyment on a Winter's evening (no telly remember), and that's what it was all about in those dark days. Mr. Strain of Brynore Hall, Criftins, retired from farming about 1950; he had surely done his whack for the war effort in more ways than one.

I remember his farm sale very well for he had a machine, called an iron horse, an engine mounted on two iron wheels. Various implements could be attached to it. In fact, it was like a two wheeled tractor without a seat, with only a pair of handles that you held on to and steered as you walked behind it. The sale had started and the auctioneer was selling and at a farm sale crowds of people gather around the auctioneer, some bidding at the various items, some watching with curiosity. This iron horse was at the end of one row of implements and someone asked Mr. Strain if it was in working order. Mr. Strain proceeded to give a demonstration. He started it up with no bother and jammed it into gear. I think that he took off across the field quicker than he anticipated. He was going at a fair old bat, engulfed in a cloud of smoke, turning at the far end heading straight back for the crowds of people around the auctioneer. About 70 yards from them, they realised that he could not stop it. They parted into two rucks as he went through he middle of them like a knife through butter. I can see him now, laughing as he came around up the field, turning at the top of the field again, when a voice said: 'Look out, he's coming back.' The machine was jammed into gear. Someone ran to it and switched the engine off and after a few more yards it spluttered to a stop with Mr. Strain completely out of breath and sweating profusely. Mopping his brow with his handkerchief he said in halting gasps: 'Well I've proved one thing — it works!'

One of my favourite characters of our village was Wynne Edwards, the Coalmerchant & Haulage Contractor. What a host of stories he had to tell, like the time when Ern. Butler was cutting his hair. Halfway through, Frank Williams came to the door shouting that his horse had just dropped dead on the road. Out of the house they shot and sure enough, the poor old horse had passed on. How true the story is of Frank's statement about the occurrence I'm not sure. It was: 'That's the first time he's done that on me.' but I do remember seeing Wynne a few days later and he said to me: 'Alfred, I had a bit of luck the other day, Frank's horse died and I had only borrowed it the day before, so I was lucky he dinna drop dead with me', and Wynne also said: 'Ern Butler dinna finish cutting my hair for another couple of days, as the both of us had forgotten where he had put the hair clippers'.

I also like the story where Charlie Roberts bought a cow at a farm sale at Dinas Mawddwy. He showed Wynne which cow he had bought. A roan cow with horns (no de-horning in those days). However, it appeared that at this sale there were two roan cows with horns. Unfortunately, Wynne must have brought the wrong one, a distance of about 40 miles. The auctioneer came to see Charlie Roberts and Wynne, and insisted that they should take the cow back free of charge, and have the other roan cow. Charlie was adamant that they had brought the right cow because he said that when she came out of the sale ring he hung his cap on one of her horns. But all to no avail. Wynne had to take her back to the farm whence she came and he did not get any payment off the auctioneer for doing it.

My Dad went for a ride with him one Summer evening. He was taking a load of furniture in his wagon to Wellington, about 30 miles away. They unloaded the furniture at a house and decided to have a drink at one of the pubs in the area. It was just at the end of the war and beer was very scarce. Wynne pulled up outside the pub window. Going into the pub they got rather a frosty welcome. My Dad ordered two pints and as the landlord pulled them, one of the local drinkers passed a sarcastic remark about the old wagon and how it was blocking the light out of the pub. Wynne heard this and told my Dad. Those two men were very dry but decided to leave having neither touched their pints nor paid for them. As they got into the wagon, Wynne said: 'We will have a drink nearer home.' To their dismay, they travelled all the way from Wellington to find that there was not another pub open all the way along the A5 back home. Wynne told me that never again would he leave a pint.

Rosie Payne had an old pram that she used to collect sticks out of Hardwick Park — bits of branches that had blown out of the trees that were growing in the Park. One day she was pushing her pram along the main road, when Brian Bebb was coming to our Smithy in a pony and trap. An army lorry, with its canvas top flapping in the wind, startled his pony and the horse bolted and hit the pram out of Rosie's hands, taking it and dragging it along the road. Brian was scared to death. Not realising the pram only contained sticks he got his pony under control and rushed back to try and assist and help with the baby, as he thought; he told me later how relieved he was after searching the pram, that the only damage that he had done was to an old pram and a few sticks.

And then the conversation came around to talk about his neighbour who had got a pony and trap, Bert Pearce of the Newns Farm, it was, and his pony could take him to Shrewsbury from Frankton in ten minutes under the hour.

Brian then went on to talk about how his Dad, Frank Bebb, had bought a new tractor on the outset of the war, and how some mornings they would find a tyre flat on the new tractor, and in time they took the tube to be mended, only to find it was not punctured. Eventually they found out that their old waggoner was coming back at night and letting the tyre down. That was his way of objecting to the introduction of tractors, and modern farming methods, and technical changes that were hastened by the war. About the start of the war Brian Bebb's Aunty Peg (Peggy Parry to me) married a lad who was a fully qualified pilot; he was called up to serve in the Royal Air Force in the very early days of the war, my Dad had made Peggy Parry a copper horse shoe for luck for her wedding. She came up to the blacksmith shop one day and requested my Dad to make her a smaller one, as her husband found difficulty in taking the larger one in his plane with him. My Dad made her a smaller horseshoe. The story goes that the first time he went up in his plane with the new smaller shoe he failed to return to base. Had the changing of the shoe changed the luck, I wonder? The odds of staying alive in the early years of the war for a pilot were very slender.

There was great excitement one day on the Perthy. Ron Jones, son of Eric Jones received news he had won a pig in a big draw. The pig eventually arrived and Ron came down to the Smithy to ask me to go and look at it, to value it. It was supposed to be worth £5 — a lot of money in those days. I went up about three days later. Looking at the pig over the pigsty door with Ron I said to him: 'How much did you say the value of the pig was supposed to be'? '£5', said Ron. 'Well,' I said, 'I inna much of a farmer, but that pig's worth at least £12.' On that Eric, Ron's Dad arrived. I passed the same remark. Both looked a little bit agitated or was it guilty. And then they both spoke together and told me the story. The organisation running the draw bought a £5 pig off a farmer and the farmer delivered it to Ron's house after dark. Putting it into the sty that night, neither of them had a good look at it. Next morning the sty was empty. Both Ron and Eric went to look for their pig; after looking for a few hours they found pigs running about by

40

Hardwick Hall in the old rockery by the gardens. There was one pig on his own, a bit away from the others. 'I bet that's your pig,' said Eric to his son, 'Let's grab him while we are here.' This they did quickly and carried the squealing, protesting pig (squealing all the way 'It inner me, It inner me') up the fields from Hardwick to their house on the Perthy, about half a mile.

Next day I was walking through Pool Cover when along the path I came across a small pig, a £5 pig, eating acorns (a diet pigs like). I quickly popped up to Ron's. Both Ron and his Dad came, caught it, quickly swopped the pigs over by putting the bigger pig into a trailer and delivering it to where it belonged at Hardwick. No one was about, and no one has been any wiser for the last thirty-five years or more, only Ron and me. But now I feel it is time to tell the story of a £5 pig.

Chapter 6

'All For A Tanner A Day'

IN the early days of the war, work was beginning to change in our little Smithy. The odd old Fordson tractor was beginning to appear on some of the local farms, the bigger ones, starting to replace the horse for some jobs. Shafts of carts were being cut off and iron draw bars were having to be made at the Smithy, so that the carts and other implements could be pulled by these cumbersome standard Fordsons. No hydraulics on them, just a clutch which you pressed down to start and right down to act as a brake (like the bumping cars at the fairground). What a transformation that was to bring to our farming community of waggoners who had only been used to horses, — then driving into the farmyard and shouting 'Wo' to the tractor! What a boom it was to blacksmiths. A horse would stop if it felt something, but not the tractor. Repairing farm implements was becoming a full time job. New technology was having to be learnt and introduced. I wonder what my grandfather would have thought; as even today I wonder what my Dad would think if he saw the change that has taken place in farming methods over the last forty years.

Artificial insemination for cows! We on our little smallholding always kept a bull for the use of the rest of the smallholdings on the Perthy so that they could bring their cows to him. My Dad used to charge 5/- for his bull, per cow, and I remember he increased it to

7/6d and one smallholder complained and said: 'Joe, do you want to become a millionaire?' But I suppose it was a 50% increase. My Dad once sold one of his cows to a neighbour and after five years it died and the buyer came and thought he should have a bit of a rebate on the deal. But now back to blacksmithing, — because livestock was not his interest.

A tractor called the Farmall was introduced from America. This was a more streamlined affair, but a very light machine. It was alright for light work like chain harrowing etc., but no good at all for lugging manure out. They would just simply rear up in the air if too much weight was put on to their back axles. There were plenty of narrow squeaks with them; to avoid more, drivers would independently lock the wheels to keep the tractor straight. Safety Officers in Wartime were unheard of. They would have needed a book as big as a church Bible to have started to write down the wrongs and rights.

Then came the introduction of the 'Fergi'. Now that really was a revolution; hydraulics, three-point linkage fitted with most of its own implements. That tractor, in my opinion, really put the seal on the working 'farm cart-horse', on many farms.

But before the departure of the farm cart-horse I remember another job that we had to do. As well as shoeing them, there was a job called frost nailing. Now this particular job used to be done after man and horse had finished their day's work at the farms, and many is the mile that I have biked around the farms on a dark winter's night to frost nail horses with only the aid of a hurricane lamp for lighting a dark stable. Now to explain what frost nailing means. What happened, with the aid of an unclencher and a pair of pincers, was that three old nails would be taken out of the shoe and three frost nails put in their place, one either side of the toe and one in the outside heel of each shoe, — a total of twelve nails for each horse.

The nails had bigger heads on them, shaped like a chisel point, to help to stop the horse from slipping when they were lugging out manure down frosty lanes into fields. They would require this job about three nights a week. When it was really frosty, one would be expected to do about ten or twelve horses a night at probably about four or five different farms. In the best kept sables the job was not too bad, but very often, one would come across the odd couple of horses where the waggoner had not cleaned the mud and snow off their legs and with the shire horses with plenty of hair on them (called feather), hands and legs would soon get very cold and wet, adding to the discomfort of a bike ride home late at night. But that was all part of the job, all part of learning the trade; when we arrived home to a good warm fire and perhaps a treat of poached eggs on toast, life did not seem too bad at all. For the record, the cost of the journey and the twelve frost nails was about 1/3d per horse.

Another hard, rough job was shoeing a young horse for the first time; or putting a pair of sale shoes onto the front feet of a colt. These were called bevelled edges and it used to be the custom that if you could nail a shoe on without a young horse getting away from you, there would be a gallon of beer extra shared out among the waggoners. There would be some cussing and hanging on to achieve that part of the bargain. The 'gentle giants' were not so gentle in those circumstances.

We bought our first motorised vehicle for Perthy Smithy in 1942. Dad paid £20 for it from Mr. Walley of Lower Frankton (later mentioned as the H.G. Lieutenant). It was an old Austin 12 car that had the back cut off from behind the front seat and the rear end made into a lorry body with pig cratches on like the modern pickup. Joe Strange had become mechanised! I was sixteen at the time and allowed to drive on a provisional licence without passing a driving test. (Tests were suspended during the war). On the steering wheel was an advance and a retard lever and a lever for accelerating with notches on.

The gear lever or gear stick had a catch on it called the gate change — to get into reverse you had to press this lever which was rather like the latch of a door. (What a difference to today's automatic gearbox, servo brakes, five speed boxes or power steering . . . . words unheard of, but I am sure they do not cause the same talking point as did our first motor car-cum-lorry.)

This vehicle started to replace our pony for jobs around the village. Coke from Ellesmere was fetched, corn from the Co-op. Lugging building materials for Hardwick Estate to the farms at Hordley, a couple of bags of cement and half a dozen barrow loads of sand and a few bricks were delivered in a quarter of the time it took old Peg, the pony.

One particular day I had been to one of the farms at Hordley and when I got back Dad was fuming. Hardly giving me time to get out of the vehicle, he told me to put the 'thing' up and not to ever take it out again until I was told! Not daring to answer back, I did just that. What had happened was that I had decided that day to see how fast this machine would go. With the wind and everything else in my favour, and with the advance and retard lever in the right place on the steering, I had reached the staggering speed of 35 m.p.h. along Hordley straight. Unbeknown to me, Charlie Wynn of Winston Farm had witnessed this historical feat and had come up to the Perthy specially to tell my Dad: 'Joe, that lad of yours will kill somebody or himself if he does not slow down'. I ask you! Thirty-five miles per hour! As I sit here writing, a car has just gone past my farm doing at least 100 m.p.h. and we think nothing of it. But I suppose the speed of a pony and trap and the speed of that vehicle of ours were in marked contrast then. It lasted us for many years and if my memory serves me right we used to have about six or eight gallons a month of petrol coupons for essential work only — none allowed for pleasure, or joy riding, and we were lucky.

I recall the first time I persuaded my Mother to come with me. It was the night we went to my Uncle Jack's at Tetchill, he was my Mother's brother who lived all of three miles away. We arrived in great excitement, Mother in her Sunday best, hat on with a hat-pin in and all. We stayed a couple of hours, and my Mother was on tenterhooks to get back before dark. I went to start up our lorry-cum-car but with no success. Not a murmur out of the engine. I swung and swung at it for a good ten minutes or so. It was the type of starting handle that was fixed on to the front of the engine. It had slipped off a couple of times and I skinned my knuckles on the front spring that jutted out from alongside the chassis. My Mother wasn't helping matters at all by saying it was the first time she had been to see her brother in her own motor car and it would be the last. My Uncle Jack by this time had gone to harness his pony up to take my Mother home, when I suddenly remembered that I had switched off the petrol tap that led from the gravity fed petrol tank under the bonnet because it leaked! I switched it back on and with a final swing of the starting handle, she roared into life. What a relief! My Mother got in and we came home in stony silence, which I felt to be far worse than if she had been shouting at me. It was many months before she ventured forth again with me. 'Pony and traps', she said were more reliable.

I remember another instance when I had a load of coke on. The clutch was slipping a bit as I tried to back up on to smithy bank. So I put her into reverse, opened the throttle out on the steering wheel, jumped out and gave her a push. As she got over the brow of the hill on to the bank, I nipped round quickly into the driving seat just in time to brake and stop her crashing into the coke ruck wall!! I could not see any danger then!!!

Many more stories could be told, but I will finish off with this one: She was getting a bit the worse for wear — radiator leaking badly, burning oil, leaving a trail of smoke behind. A welding instructor who was teaching me asked Dad whether I could take an engine for him to Dowley's Garage at Shrewsbury. Filling up about four or five gallon drums with water from the well, away we went, stopping every five miles or so to top up whenever it came up to boiling point, showing on the gauge on top of the radiator outside the bonnet. You could see it starting to get hot as you were travelling along. Arriving at Shrewsbury with nearly all the water gone, we unloaded the engine and I filled our drums up with water for the journey back to Frankton, about 18 miles away. Coming to the level-crossing at Harlescott, I had to wait for a train, which meant more precious water leaking out of the radiator. After the train had passed I crashed her into gear and one of the five-gallon drums overbalanced and started to roll about on the back of our little lorry-cum-car. I decided that I dare not stop for a hundred yards or so. I kept going but to my dismay met workers leaving Chatwood Safe Factory, many on push-bikes, some on foot.

There seemed to be hundreds of them. That was when the five-gallon drum of water departed over the back of the lorry heading straight for the bikes, but luckily missing them all by inches. I did not know what to do, so I decided to choose the coward's way, I kept going! They might have thought it was a depth charge or something like that, even Hitler's secret weapon! I now had only sufficient water to get as far as Cockshutt, so I filled up there again

46

and eventually arrived back at the Perthy in one piece. The journey to Shrewsbury and back had taken something like five hours — a distance of 32 miles. I smile and think that in those days we thought that Shrewsbury and Wrexham were in another world and that it would take a week of planning to go there for something or other. (London? never 'eard of the place.) Today, twenty minutes in an average car. Ah well! We managed to solder the radiator so that it did not leak too badly and the old girl kept on going right up until the end of the war. I recall she did one important run after that, — another story, another chapter.

One day in the smithy, an old lad, coming through the door from the front into the main shop dropped a new ounce of tobacco out of his waistcoat pocket, but was not aware he had done so. Dad had seen what had happened and gave the tobacco a kick into the front and picked it up unbeknown to the old lad. About twenty minutes later, my Dad said: 'Bill, can you spare me a pipeful of tobacco?' 'John Peel isn't it?' Dad added, — to rub it in.

'I have just got a new ounce from the Top Shop' Bill replied graciously, and he started to feel in his waistcoat pocket for his ounce of John Peel. I can see him now, — he got quite in a panic searching all his pockets.

'Where the hell have I put it?' My Dad and I kept quiet and straight faced. 'Damn me, I must have dropped it between here and the Top Shop.' and took off before we had time to stop him. All the way back he went, looking for the tobacco. About half an hour later, he came back into the shop. 'Well Joe, my ration for three days gone,' was all he could say. My Dad then handed him the 'bacca and told him that it had dropped out in the smithy and fell between the horseshoes. The relief on old Bill's face I can see now. They filled their pipes and had a smoke.

Tom Hughes, the estate bricklayer, had a habit of always putting his clay pipe on the anvil and my Dad used to say to him:

'Blast you Tom, canna yo put it somewhere else out of my way?' But he still persisted, everytime he came into the shop.

One day, my Dad, tired of telling him not to put his pipe on the anvil gave it a sharp tap with the hammer. No need to describe what happened, and I won't repeat what Tom Hughes said, but he never put his clay pipe on the anvil again.

47

In times when most farm vehicles had wooden wheels, hooping was an important part of a blacksmith's craft and it had its own well tried procedure. The wooden wheels would go rotten, and the iron bands (or hoops) would be taken off. Eric Jones the joiner and wheelwright would put in new spokes and new felles. Often he would have to make a complete new wheel. Making spokes and felles etc., was a really skilled trade. Dad used to like to hoop about fifteen to twenty wheels at the same time, so only using one fire. It was quite a big day in the life of a blacksmith, and many a time I have seen Eric Jones running down the Perthy from his shop to ours with a cartwheel 5 feet high, bowling it like a bowler. The weight would be about 2 cwt. (What price a modern car if one of those was to hit it? Of course there were very few cars on the road then, perhaps two a day).

Wheels of all sorts and sizes would be assembled in our smithy. Then, our job would be to sort them out and start making the hoops the right size for the wheels. In fact you had to make it smaller than the wheel because when iron gets hot it expands and when it is cooled off it contracts, hence tightening on to the wheel. On a big heavy 6" wide by $\frac{1}{2}$" thick and say 5 feet across you would make it about $1\frac{1}{2}$" to 2" smaller than the wheel so that it would tighten and bring all the felles and spokes together. The iron hoops would be laid out in an organised pile, big hoops on the outside, smallest one in the middle. Logs and turf would be placed round them, some old hedge brushings that had been dried would be lit and placed around to get an even fire going.

Extra logs would also be ready to put on different places in the fire as the others burnt away. It really seemed quite disorganised but it was just the opposite in fact. Don't forget, a good week's work was at stake in the next hour or two. Water would be all ready fetched from the pit into an old tank up near where the hoops would eventually be put on. The hooping would be timed for when the men from Hardwick Estate knocked off work. Dai Phillips, Jack Prodger, Fred Gregory would be 'enlisted', and my Mother would also help. Dad would be prowling around, looking at the fire, estimating how hot the different hoops were. With a final look he would pronounce the time was right, and he'd make sure that everyone knew what they were about. The men would nod, and then it would start.

Dad, with a long iron-stailed fork, would lift up the first hoops. Two of the men would slide a long piece of piping under the hoop, lifting at the same time, then, with my Dad walking backwards away from the fire, the hoop would be placed on the ground near to the wheel that was to be hooped. The men would let go of the piping and grab the hoop with a pair of long iron tongs, lift it again and place it onto the wheel. It would then be levered down with tools called 'dogs', making sure that the nail holes came into the middle of the felles, not the spoke. As soon as the hoop was on, we lads, with our buckets of water, would cool it as quickly as possible, then the next wheel would be put in its place, — the Perthy version of a production line.

The same procedure would then take place until all the hoops were out of the fire and on the wheels. If everything went right, we would hoop about twelve to fifteen wheels in about half-an-hour. Speed was essential. The hoop would only go on if it was very hot. Most hooping days went fairly smoothly, although pretty hectic. Occasionally a hoop was missed, either because it was not hot enough or maybe a wrong measurement had been taken. When that happened, tempers would become frayed. Hammers would fly. You would get in one another's way, everybody blaming somebody else, — it really would be chaos. Eventually, it would be put on one side to be removed, altered and re-heated after the other hoops had been done. As the last hoop was done, out would come the home-brew, bread, cheese and pickles. I can see the scene now. Men and lads sitting down on various bits of wood or on their haunches, faces as black as soot, but glowing with satisfaction knowing that we had helped to hoop wheels on Joe Strange's smithy bank. No payment was expected, — the men knew full well that my Dad would pay them back in kind; lend them the pony and trap for their bit of hay harvest or to take the kids for a ride in the evenings. The barter system was in operation again, and as I look back at the prices charged for hooping a wheel, the amount of time, energy and skill, yes, real skill, no wonder there was going to be a shortage of blacksmiths.

All the refreshments would have been made by my Mother. This reminds me of how my Mother used to help in the Smithy and how many farmers' wives helped out on the farms. One night Frank

Davies from Berghill Farm came to the house and said that he was sending two young unbroken cart-horses to the Smithy next day with the Waggoner. The Waggoner turned out to be his wife, she had brought these two young cart-horses about $2\frac{1}{2}$ miles including about a mile of main road to the Smithy to be shod on her own. For a first class farm chap to have brought one would of been considered an achievement or brave act, but for a woman to have brought two of them must surely go down as one of the bravest feats ever accomplished by a woman. I wonder what the present day farmer's wife would think or say at being asked to do such a task.

Not long after the war started my Dad bought all the horse-drawn vehicles from Hardwick Hall. In all I think that there were about eight to ten of them. The small dog cart / the cart / the float / the trap / the governess cart / the four-wheel harvest wagon / the four wheel carriage and the six wheeled carriage that used to take the gentry to catch the train at Shrewsbury. If my memory serves me right, he gave about £12 for all those vehicles.

Now to tell you what he did with them. Well, he fetched them home, one at a time, with old Peg the pony. What a sight they were, all in a row on Smithy Bank. They were all in first class order. He started to dismantle them one at a time. The wheels were taken off, then the springs and the axles. The woodwork was knocked off and put in to rucks to be burned for hooping wheels, this was near sacrilege. Axles were made into wedges for splitting trees. The springs were to be used for making main leaves for the old motor-car . . . . Yes, I have made many a new car spring out of an old carriage spring.

Quite a few of the vehicles had trap lamps on them. I think many of those were given away. The rest of the ironwork was straightened out and made into various stays to repair other farm implements. What a price those carriages etc., today? I could not even guess their value except to say it would be in the thousands of pounds. I remember saying to my Dad later on that it was a shame that he had not built a shed and put them all in. His reply was: 'What would the cost of the shed be?' Of course, we can all be clever with hind-sight. He pointed out that he needed the ironwork off them to make a living, everything was in such short supply. I suppose he was right really at the time, but I often think what a tragedy it was that all those lovely old carriages were smashed up. But he was once, at least, the owner of a complete set of horse-drawn carriages, and I suppose really that's what makes an antique.

I remember Tom Williams who had a blacksmith's business in Birkenhead, having the folding steps off one of the vehicles to put on one at Birkenhead. What happened to it I don't know. Tom Williams (whom we used to call Uncle Tom) retired from shoeing street horses at Birkenhead when he was 68. He bought himself a little Morris Minor and had four years of retirement and then at the age of 72 decided to re-open the village smithy at Thornton Hough on the Wirral, shoeing horses there for another four years. Early retirement, redundancy payments? What were they? The smith at Thornton Hough had a smithy door in the shape of a horse-shoe. When Tom Williams came for a few days holiday to Frankton, my Dad and he visited Jack Pearce at Oswestry, who had a smithy near the traffic lights. His brother, Jim Pearce, had one at Four Lane Ends by West Felton. I think that they came from the Birkenhead district to this area. Sadly both smithies are now closed.

Instead of always using matches to light his pipe, Dad would get a red hot cinder out of the smithy fire, place it on the top of his pipe, puff away and when his pipe was lit, flick the cinder back on to the fire. One young lad who had watched him many times doing that, went home and said to his Dad, who was filling his pipe with tobacco, 'Why don't you smoke cinders like Mr. Strange?'

One evening Ron Hodnet from Lower Ridge Farm and I were up in the top end of our little village kicking our heels and thinking what to do when we realised that one of the houses in Bottle Row had not got a light on, nor was there any smoke coming out of the chimney. We then remembered that Mrs. Colesby was away staying with her sister, Mrs. Malam, at Loppington. In between the row of houses was an entrance, and with the low roof which the houses had it meant that one could easily get on to the roof by the chimney. Finding a big old slate and some clod of earth, we proceeded to block the top of Alf Colesby's chimney, knowing that he would soon be done from his round as an insurance man, and would light his fire. The plan worked well, Mr. Colesby came home lit the fire and the picture that I have of him was his coming out of his house

51

coughing and choking because his house was full of smoke. We were away across the shop fields.

To the best of my knowledge this is the first time that this story has been told, it is really a wonder that no one saw us. Heaven help us had someone done so; goodness knows what the punishment would have been. At the age of 60, I agree it deserved more than a telling off; it was a rotten thing to do. But even a blacksmith has to let himself go, at times.

One night towards the end of the war, when I was a teenager, I was on my way to chapel. Mrs. Walley had been a staunch chapelgoer for all the years that she lived in Frankton, so that after she died her five sons paid to have electricity and lights installed in the Top Chapel in memory of their mother. (What the cost was then I did not know, but I suppose it would be well over £1,000 today). I remember the switching-on occasion very well — the chapel was always full for do's like that. A truly fitting gesture in memory of one that had done so much for the Top Chapel; now back to the night I was going to chapel on my own. A big car pulled up and a voice said: 'Are you a Strange?' I said, 'I am.' 'Well,' said the voice 'My name's Walley, one of Mrs. Walley's sons.' He continued, 'I was going to chapel myself tonight but I have had an urgent message for me to get back to my farm at Wolverhampton. If you are going to chapel will you do me a favour and put this pound note in the collection for me?' I know if you're a Strange I can trust you to do that.' 'Certainly,' I said, and away he drove. 'A pound note,' I thought. 'More than I put away in a year.' The normal collection at that time would have been a penny from children and about sixpence from grown ups. Sitting in chapel with the pound note tucked safely in my pocket, I thought, 'I won't say who it is from until we are coming out of chapel.' Mr. Tom Lewis of Lower Frankton was the treasurer and he always counted the collection. I can see now the look of amazement and bewilderment on his face. He looked all around the chapel trying to fathom out who it was that had been so generous, but alas only the same villagers were there. I left him pondering for a moment or so, then I went and told him the full story, as to how he came to find a pound note on the collecting plate.

Chapter 7

'To be a Farrier's Boy'

AFTER working for my Father for two years (and obviously knowing more than he did!) he said to me one night: 'I have been having a word with Dave Evans,' (the blacksmith from Ellesmere, who gave Grandma Strange her only motor-bike ride), 'and I think it will be as well if you go and give 'im a hand on Mondays, Wednesdays and Fridays, and tell 'im all you know! O.K.?' I did. I had no choice. Little did I know what was in store for me for the next three years or so. These two had got together and made arrangements for their shoeing. Dave was to arrange his shoeing for Monday, Wednesday and Friday, and my Dad his for Tuesday, Thursday and Saturday, which literally meant I was practically living under horses for the next three years. What an education! Very often when the threshing box was in the area they would, between them, lend me out to farmers to do a day's work for them. By this time many farmers were short staffed due to the call-up of younger men into the forces. Give me the shoeing of horses anytime to a day's threshing though, but more about that later.

Friday, being market day, meant farmers coming in leaving their horses and carts, ponies and traps at Dave's stable. It didn't take me long to find out who were the most generous when you gave them a hand to harness up their ponies to go home at various times of the day, many with a few drinks inside them. On a good Friday

I could make 5/- loading them up, handing them the reins, taking them out on to the street, pointing them in their different directions, knowing full well that the horse would do the rest. Cross Street in Ellesmere had never been heard of as 'one-way'. I shall always remember one farmer. If I got his horse ready for him before he arrived, so he could make a quick getaway, I could be on for 2/6d tip (a quarter of my week's wages).

Ellis Miner was a coalman who used to have his horse shod regularly at Dave's shop. The big old cart-horse was very quiet to shoe. The only snag was that he would never arrive until after his own day's work. A set of caulk and wedge shoes would only last him about 17 days as he was always on the road. Overtime payment? What was that? In those days there were about three or four street-horses, — Jack Powell and Arthur Ackroyd used to lug coal from the station to the dairy down Wharf Road, five or six loads a day. Cross Street has been a 'one-way' street only since the war which means that you now have to go all around the town, a much longer journey.

As I got more experienced in shoeing, I could tell by the noise that shoes made on the street how close they were to needing a new set. If at about five o'clock one could hear a 'tinny' sound coming down Cross Street and slowing down outside the smithy you knew you would be late knocking off! If that particular day you wanted to be home early, you would say under your breath, 'Keep going you bugger,' but often to no avail. 'No arguing, get stuck in', Dave would shout. The first horse that I ever shod on my own was at Dave's shop. A young three-year-old colt owned by Jim Nicholls of Elson Farm. About four days later he came into the yard at Dave' shop and said that his horse was lame. I felt terrible. Dave went out on his motor-bike and side-car to see the horse. I thought that I would be blamed for inexperience, but, thank God, it was nothing to do with the shoeing. I was so relieved at the time that I can't even remember what the cause was.

Close to Dave Evans's shop in the same yard was Sleigh's carpenters and undertakers shop. Gaffer Sleigh was the boss — well, that was what we called him. His real name was Jack and had many tales to tell. One day as I was boiling the kettle on the smithy fire, for our morning mug of tea, he came in and commented on the state of the big enamel jug that I used to make the tea in. 'To be quite honest, I thought the true colour of it was black,' he said. 'I'll give it a wash in the bosh' — (the bosh is the name for the cast iron trough that holds water at the back of the smithy fire to cool a piece of casting called a Tue Iron that carries on into the middle of the fire from the bellows. (All that sounds like the house that Jack (Sleigh) built.)

When he did give it a wash, the colour of the jug was duck-egg blue! I looked in amazement. I made the tea in the nice clean jug. It tasted terrible. The remarks and comments I received from the other workers in the yard as to the different taste of the tea I dare not repeat. It was some weeks before the taste of the tea got back to normal. Believe me or believe me not, I have never been able to drink another cup of tea from that day to this.

What a character Gaffer Sleigh was. Sometimes he would say, if my shoes were dirty: 'Alfie, have you lost your boot brushes?' or 'Who cleaned your shoes this morning?' His own shoes were probably as dirty as mine. This went on for months until one morning he passed the same remark: 'Have you lost your shoe brushes Alfie?' 'I have and it dunna seem that you have found them in Cambrian Avenue either!' I replied. He laughed and said that I was growing up.

Another of his habits was to borrow tuppence to go and make a 'phone call. This I would do and possibly later in the day, he would give me the tuppence back. Two days later I would say to him: 'Gaffer, you owe me tuppence from the other day.' 'Dinna I give it you?' he would say. 'No you anna', I would reply. 'Oh, I am sorry', and he would give me another tuppence. Honest — robbery! Some times he would say when he wanted change for the 'phone call: 'Give us tuppence Alfie for this sixpence'. It used to pay me to have change ready for him.

What a man he was. He had a contract with the Polish Hospital at Penley to make coffins. A lot of the Polish soldiers had, I believe, been injected with a T.B. germ by order of Hitler and were dying at the rate of eight to ten every week. It was a tragic affair, but I suppose Gaffer Sleigh had seen so many deaths that he became really quite hardened to it. There were also Polish Officers there dying from different illnesses. As was the Polish custom they were buried in full military uniform, and one day Gaffer said to me: 'Alfie, what size shoes do you take? I'm burying a Polish Officer tomorrow.'

I said I would not be able to wear shoes like that. Whether he was joking or not, I am not sure but I thank Gaffer Sleigh for giving me a couple of years of country education — the sort you cannot get out of books.

Harry Barkley worked at Jack Sleigh's shop at the time that I was there. He came from Criftins and was a terrific character. He was getting on a bit and many were the stories he had to tell of his younger days. A keen supporter of local football, I believe at one time he was involved in burying the village cup, for what reason I don't know. His great love was ponies. He used to break them in and race them at local meetings. My favourite story about him is the one about a pony he owned called Dolly Grey.

This pony was a flier and would have won everything she was entered for, but for one great failing, she would not, or could not turn while racing. In the straight, no problem, but come a bend and straight on she used to go, taking all in her way. Harry had a bright idea as the Whit Monday Sports Day at Ellesmere approached. A feature of the day was the evening horse-racing on a field at the rear of the United Dairies. It was one of the highlights of the year for us and neighbouring villages. Harry enlisted the support of a lot of young men to help him win a race with Dolly Grey. His plan was that on a sharp bend before the last straight, they were to be lined across the corner where Dolly Grey always used to run out, armed with flags, jackets, bags and any item that could be seen and used to make her turn. But to no avail, Dolly Grey, as usual, miles in front of the other horses went through the line of lads as if they were not there. Past the sewerage beds, finishing up among the hobby-horses on the fairground. Who knows what greatness she could have achieved if only she could have turned a corner properly. Harry left me with wonderful memories of him and my working days at Dave Evans's blacksmith shop. To the best of my knowledge, one of Dolly Grey's shoes is still hanging up at the Fox at Criftins.

Les Johnson was a local waggoner at Edwards's of Colemere Woods Farm in those days. What a treat to shoe his horses. They were always immaculately turned out, even to come to the smithy. Their manes would be plaited and they always looked fit enough and smart enough to go into any show. Les Johnson had an infectious laugh and could 'take off' a lot of the local farmers' sayings. As I write this about him I hear that he has passed away. There doesn't seem to be the Les Johnsons and the Harry Barkleys and the Jack Sleigh's and the Dave Evans's about today. A pity really. They had so much to tell the young people like me then. What you could learn from them in an hour or two of their company would fill a dozen books.

Another job we had to do at Dave's was welding the Gas Yard rakes. Mr. Butler and Mr. Davies were working there then and the one requiring regular repairs was used to rake clinkers out of the bottom of the fires. The heat was quite terrific and used to burn the ends off the rake. This would always be a rush job — just before knocking-off time as a rule. Alan Ashley, the boss from the gasworks, used to ride up on his bike to see Dave about different things.

On my way to work at Dave's one morning, I stopped to put one of Reeves, the Buildings Farm, heifers back in a field. This made me five minutes late for work— belting through the square at five minutes past eight instead of five minutes to eight. Rushing into the yard, Dave had already got the Smithy fire blown up — the first job every morning — before I had a chance to explain why I was late, he said: 'Well, and who lied on your shirt this morning?' Pointless to say why!

Those were the days when time was time. It did not matter being late knocking off in the evening, but to be late in the morning was a real crime and a disgrace. In those days I had already done a couple of hours work at our own little smallholding before cycling to Ellesmere a good two miles away. I smile at the hours that people seem to start today. Tea breaks, rest days, finishing Friday lunch-time until eight o'clock Monday morning, and still many go past my farm allowing themselves only the barest of time to get to their place of work. I still say one of the pleasures of life is to be able to do a day's work for a day's pay and I am sure that understanding the need of a day's work to enable him to employ labour and give service to his customer will still prove to be best. Dave Evans was a hard boss, but a fair one, speaking from experience of working for him for three years. He would be on time himself of a morning, so why shouldn't his workers? I feel grateful to Dave Evans for teaching me the craft of a farrier and blacksmith.

I add a few more stories of my own experiences of working for Dave. One involves a horse called Jock, a big cart-horse who did not like his feet picked up by the normal method. You had to tap his hooves with a hammer, — he would then pick his foot up and you grabbed the hoof with your hands. Nobody told me this and the first time I tried to shoe him I tried to lift his hind hoof up in the normal way, only to find myself kicked and shoved into the coke outside — a distance of about ten yards. It was a common trick to be played on any new apprentice, not to tell them the different whim of horses. Find out by your own mistakes and you learn a lot quicker that way, was the motto — ('restrictive practice'?).

Another day, a complete stranger came in, much the worse for drink. From out of the shoeing place at Dave's to the bottom shop where the shoes were made ready, were two steps. This character stood swaying on the top step for a second or two and then fell forward. He missed hitting his head on the anvil by a hair's breadth as he crumbled to the floor. Had he hit his head on the anvil it surely would have killed him. Jack Sleigh remarked it was a pity the anvil was not a bit closer to the steps. One thing, we would not have had far to take him to be measured up at Sleigh's undertaking shop.

Dave smoked Woodbines during the war years, but keeping him supplied was quite a job! Someone would come into the shop and say Alice Crowther had some in, or Bob Walker or Miss Timms (Kiosk along the Mere side) or the Co-op. Away I'd go on my bike, lucky to come back with 20 to keep him happy for another day or so. Perhaps I would be extra lucky and buy an ounce of 'twist' for Dad as well. It was a full time job getting their fags and bacca.

One day we shod a gypsy's horse and he refused to pay. He said it was too dear. 'Well,' said Dave, 'I'm not bothered,' starting to take the shoes off. He paid. The local gypsies were alright, — it was those travelling through the district that were a problem.

The time was now approaching for me to leave Dave and come back home to work full-time for my Dad. But as I look back to those years of my apprenticeship, I think what a good job my Dad had the wisdom to send me to where I had a boss I could look up to. Many of the lessons I learned helped me through my own life as the village blacksmith.

Both Dave and Dad would hire me out to help farmers with threshing. John Tom Thomas was the main contractor in the area, as I remember. He had quite a few boxes and one regular driver was called Albert. He used to drive the old type steam engine. What a skill and a work of art, driving and setting up in a muddy and uneven stack-yard was. This was normally done the evening before or early morning. The threshing box would be drawn up alongside the Dutch barn or stack, with either a big old type wire baler at the back, or a chopper, whichever the farmer wanted. (Some wanted their straw baled, and some wanted it chopped.)

There would always be plenty of dust and straw flying around. Throats would be as dry as a fish within half an hour. The noise and roar of the drum of the box and steam engine were such that you could hardly hear shouts. At dinnertime the farmer would point to his mouth with his fingers, such was the noise. Pay was 5/- a day plus dinner or 7/6d a day — bring your own butties.

Some men would follow the machines from farm to farm and sleep in the farm buildings. Mourners, they were called. A particular character I remember was Shropshire Bill. He seemed to be at all the farms I went to and was always a bit naggy, it seemed to me. Once I recall I was on the bay pitching sheaves of corn. This was fairly easy early in the day because you were pitching sheaves downhill on to the box. The lad cutting the strings off the sheaves was called the bond cutter. The feeder, he was the man who fed the loose sheaves into the thresher, the drum of which was spinning around at a great rate. Usually the feeder was Shropshire Bill.

As the day wore on pitchers' work got harder because they were starting to pitch the sheaves uphill. This day, Jeff Williams from Criftins and I were pitching the sheaves at Harold Price from Onston Farm, Tetchill. We were getting a bit tired and Bill was shouting at us to keep working. We pushed on a bit and got about twenty sheaves on to the platform leading to the feeder, Shropshire Bill, Jeff and I watched in dismay as he deliberately nudged them back on to the floor of the bay. I looked at him in disgust and he had a sneering look on his face. I shouted at him what an awkward beggar he was, knowing he could not hear. He made signals with his fingers what he thought of us as we pitched the sheaves of corn that he had knocked down. After the day was over I told Jeff I would 'get him tomorrow'.

Next day, after about an hour, the chance came. We had just started another bay and were pitching the sheaves at about the same level as the top of the threshing box. I selected a nice tight sheaf on the end of my pikel, took careful aim. My aim was true and the corn hit Bill sideways. His old peaked cap came off and zoomed down the drum and into the thresher. He jumped off the threshing box on to the bay of corn and came for me like a madman. I am sure he would have killed me if he caught me, but I was away, down the side of the bay and across the yard. I knew he could not catch me then — I was too fast for him. After a while, peace was restored and he was persuaded to get back to his job. As I went back to the bay, his hat came out all in pieces in a bale of straw.

I kept my distance from him afterwards, but he never again pitched sheaves of corn back off the threshing box. Rats were quite a plague those days and sometimes as you got lower down the bay, you could feel the sheaves moving under your feet. On most farms they had a couple of terrier dogs. Wire-netting would be placed round the outside of the bay so that the rats could not escape and it would not be unusual for as many as thirty or forty rats to be killed at the end of a day's threshing.

One of the stories Albert told was of the time he and his mate had been to The Fox at Bagley, arriving back to sleep in one of the lofts. On the other side of the road was Hordley Churchyard. One of the farm lads brought them supper up to the loft, when Albert said he could hear voices. They listened and heard: 'One for you, one for me, one for you, one for me . . .' 'What are they doing?' asked the farm lad. 'I dunno,' said Albert, 'But it could be the Devil and the Lord counting out the souls in the Churchyard.' Albert told me it was a funny thing — the lad was off like a flash down the granary steps as if the Devil was after *him*. The fact was that two more farm lads were sharing out chestnuts and apples they had pinched in one of the stables under the loft.

Land Army girls were now appearing on the farms. Some were town girls, but I was too young at the time to take much notice of them, and their motto of 'Backs to the Land' meant nothing to me!

A lot of them did however marry country lads. One elderly farmer in the district had a visit from a Ministry of Agriculture official. She told him that his one and only farm worker had to join up and was to be replaced by a Land Girl. After the forms were signed and the ministry woman was preparing to drive out of his gateway in her car, he called after her. She stopped and he said: 'This Land Girl I am having to live in. Can you tell me what I can find her to do in the daytime?'

Coming home from Ellesmere one night after working late at Dave's, my red rear light was an old type paraffin lamp. I did not bother to light it on leaving Ellesmere. About a mile out of Ellesmere, by Newnes Farm, a policeman shouted to me to 'stop', which I did. 'Where is your back light,' he asked. 'I lit it when I left Ellesmere,' was my reply. Putting his hand on the lamp he said: 'In that case, it should be warm, but it's stone cold.' It lit when he struck a match. I wonder if he ever became Chief Constable!

I was still working half-time for Dave Evans when Frank Bebb of Newnes Farm came one Friday to my Dad's Smithy and said: 'Joe, if I send a set of harrows up tonight, could you have them sharpened and ready for Monday?' 'Well,' my Dad said, 'I'm very busy, but I'll do my best.' After he had gone I said to my Dad (I had just got back from Ellesmere). 'If you give me 10/- for doing those harrows, I will do them for you.' 'Alright,' said Dad. 'I will give you 10/-, but you do them in your own time not mine.' That meant Saturday afternoon, but I was desperate for that 10/- note. I had made arrangements to meet a lass in Oswestry, and take her to first house pictures at the Regal, then to a Dance at the Baths, — total cost for two about 10/-. My Dad would be getting about £1/10s. (£1.50p) for sharpening those harrows, sixty at 6d apiece. I started at about 6.30 on Friday night, as soon as Mr. Bebb brought them, knocking off at about 11 p.m., I was up next morning at 6, worked for my Dad until about 2 p.m. then on the harrows until about 10 p.m. on Saturday, finishing them off late on Sunday after Chapel — all in my own time. Frank Bebb fetched them on Monday and was pleased to have them done. 'Thanks Joe,' he said.

After he had gone I said to Dad: 'Don't forget, I would like that 10/- note for Saturday.' 'Alright,' was his reply. Come Saturday afternoon no sign of my money and it was time to get ready to catch the 5 p.m. bus to Oswestry for my night out with this girl. I plucked up courage and said to my Dad: 'Can I have my 10/- for doing them harrows?' He was silent for a while then he looked at me and said: 'I've been thinking, as Frank Bebb has a quarterly account with me he won't be getting a bill for those harrows for another two months.' 'Although he is a good payer it could be twelve weeks before I get paid, so I'll pay you then.' My face dropped. Bang went my night out to the pictures and Dance at the Baths in Oswestry. It was no good asking Mother, Dad had made his decision and that was it. I don't know who that girl married but if she happens to read this, I do apologise for not turning up on that Saturday night in 1943.

It was just another part of country blacksmithing practice and learning the hard lessons of life. Dad was right, really, and to the best of my knowledge, I don't think I ever did get that 10/- note for the harrows.

A remark he once made to my Mother when he had gone to a Blacksmith's Meeting in Oswestry with his son, Bill's best shoes on, when Bill wanted the shoes to go out himself, my Mother said to him when he came home: 'Joe, what did you want to wear Bill's best shoes for?' His reply was: 'He has worn many a pair of mine.' I can add no further to that only to say that I now know what he meant.

My career nearly ended before it began. I came in from the Frankton Parish Hall one night. Mother had gone to bed, only Dad was up. I could see that he was upset. 'Sit down,' he said, 'and tell me the truth.' 'Did you at any time ill treat or kick a pony that was shod today?' 'Never,' I said. 'But the pony was difficult to shoe, which I could never understand, because it was always quiet and had never given any trouble.' Then he said: 'I believe you, but we have been reported to the R.S.P.C.A. by the owner of the pony, for ill-treating it over shoeing. She also said we have lamed the pony in every foot.'

Next day the R.S.P.C.A. Officer arrived very officiously, and said he was taking the Case to Court. Both Dad and I were adamant that we were not to blame, and we both said that it was unusual for the pony not to stand quiet while it was being shod; and I said that the pony seemed to be in some sort of pain when we tried to pick his feet up.

The lady owner however was determined that I should be prosecuted. She was only willing to listen to the evidence of an eleven year old girl who I now honestly believe said on the spur of the moment I had kicked and ill-treated the pony. Eventually we were summoned to attend Court at Ellesmere.

The lady who had taken me to Court had been trying to get other people to say that I had ill-treated their horses as well, but all to no avail. I said to my Dad we ought to take her to Court for trying to take away my character. He however would not, he said: 'If you tell the truth everything will always come out right for you.' The following words are a record as to how the Court Case went. I will not enlarge on that, but often I have wondered what my career would have been had the ruling gone against me.

THE FARRIERS JOURNAL (AUGUST 1946)

Correspondence

ALLEGED CRUELTY TO A PONY

A case was heard at a Magistrates Court, at Ellesmere (Shrops.), on July 8th, in which Mr. Strange, Junr., a young man of 20 was charged with cruelty to a pony by kicking it, while shoeing the pony on June 15th.

It appeared the pony was brought to be shod by a little girl of 11 years, an accomplished young rider, and although the pony had previously always been quiet, on this occasion it was very upset and restive, giving considerable trouble. Later the same day, lumps or swellings were noticed, and the girl alleged that Mr. Strange had ill-treated the pony. A veterinary surgeon and the local R.S.P.C.A. Inspector were sent for and a prosecution by the Society was decided upon. Giving evidence the veterinary surgeon said the swellings were consistent with kicking, but admitted they could have been caused by a blunt instrument, stating that the pony was even at the date of the Court suffering from the effects of the alleged ill-treatment.

For the defence Mr. Strange stoutly maintained that he did not kick the pony, or ill-use it in any way. Mr. Strange, Senr., confirmed this, stating that he had carried on business at his Smithy between 40 and 50 years without a complaint of this nature; during the whole of this time he never countenanced or allowed horses to be knocked about. A witness stated he was present for at least half-an-hour while the pony was being shod and although it was difficult to shoe, it was not ill-used.

Another witness, passing by, stated that she saw the pony 'rearing and carrying on' outside the Forge and remarked to a friend that they (the Stranges), looked like having a difficult job to shoe it.

Although not included in the charge, the owner had accused Mr. Strange of laming the pony, insisting that it was 'pricked' in every foot, ordering Mr. Strange, Senr., to take off all the shoes, which he did. With the owners consent, on July 2nd, Mr. C. Richardson, F.W.C.F. of Shrewsbury, examined the pony's feet and stated in Court that on that date it was quite sound, and there was no reason why the shoes could not be put on again.

The Chairman said the evidence was conflicting and the Bench had come to the conclusion that the summons had not been proved, and it would be dismissed.

Mr. F. S. Butter, Whitchurch, instructed by the Association solicitors, very ably defended the case, and it was certainly not the fault of Mr. J. C. Gittins, Oswestry, that the prosecution failed to prove their case.

On the same day, after the Court, another farrier was requested to shoe the pony, but refused. Next day, the mother of the little girl witness, and the lady owner of the pony, interviewed the Stranges, very humbly apologising for the trouble and upset caused, and begging them to shoe it. It was mutually decided to forgive and forget whereupon Mr. Strange and his son re-shod the pony, thus showing a very creditable spirit after an action which, had it succeeded, might have ruined the career of a young, promising rural blacksmith.

Obviously my character and my capability as a farrier would have been taken away and I would not have been the Village Blacksmith for 40-odd years had I not been believed. I know also that my Dad's pride would have been very hurt. He had been Village Blacksmith for 40-odd years, and his father before him.

A few weeks after the Court Case we found fresh evidence that the pony in question had been involved in a jumping accident the day before it had come to be shod, hence the fact that it was difficult to shoe. Dad could have gone for the lady who took us to Court, to claim damages from her and her husband. But he

Frankton's first Cricket Pavilion

Hardwick Pool

Tom Speake outside his cottage

Welsh Frankton Parish Hall

The tree and the shed

1936 Ford-Eight

Author's wedding, 1951

Football team 1950

Frankton Cricket Team, 1950

Author, 21 years of age

would not; he said: 'They have humbly apologised, that's good enough for me.'

Dad passed away about twelve months later. I have always admired him for his action; in that incident, he truly conducted himself in an honest and upright way, and I am glad he went to his grave without the slightest doubt of his skill nor stain on his character as the Village Blacksmith.

So I believe that in that story there is a lesson for everyone — 'Get your facts right before you accuse or blame anyone. Truth will always prevail.'

Since the Abdication in 1936 (suddenly made topical again by the death of the Duchess of Windsor). I have had it preached to me that it takes a quarter of a century to build up goodwill — but it can be shattered overnight by one disastrous incident.

As part of my apprenticeship with Dave Evans, I had extraneous duties. The 'phone would go, the operator would tell Dave, Leading Fireman in the Ellesmere Fire Service, 'Fire,' and Dave would shout to *me*: 'Go, ring the fire-bell,' to summon all the firemen within hearing distance to turn out. He said all of that at first, later it was — 'Bell, Alf, quick.'

The bell was in an old wooden frame above the roof of the Fire Station next to Tims Garage at that time. You had to be careful not to tug too hard in case it came crashing down. Men would appear from everywhere, some on bikes, some running, some out of the 'blue', it seemed. I can't remember any in cars — but then there wouldn't be, only farmers and doctors and such had petrol. What a sight! Joe Butler coming round Lloyds Bank Corner and down Cross Street on his bike! It's a wonder he never knocked anyone down. If he could have gone in the Whit Monday bike race, on the Wharf Meadow, there is no knowing what fame he might have achieved. Ten years earlier, they would have had more time, — because the Leading Fireman would have been running round the field trying to catch the horse.

Dave Evans came to work one morning all smiles, 'Well,' he said, 'Lena has given birth to a son, and he was born with a hammer in each hand, so surely he is destined to be a blacksmith.' Which is the case, as his son succeeded his Dad. Dave's words have been proved true.

Chapter 8

'Frankton's Own Dad's Army'

IN a previous chapter, I referred to Frankton's Home Guard. At first they used to wear arm-bands stamped L.D.V. The first recollection I have of the Local Defence Volunteers was the night Whittington Home Guard to-be were doing a practice, defending the canal bridge on the main road at the bottom of Gannow Hill. A gang of Frankton lads had gone to watch this first real exercise of the war. We were on the Whittington side of the bridge when a voice said: 'Which side of this bridge do you lads belong?' 'Frankton,' we said. 'Right, you have ten seconds or you'll have to show your identity cards,' said the voice.

As we ran back over the bridge we saw someone putting on his arm-band. He had a gun with him, which was not a proper rifle and one of us asked how far would his gun kill. He said: 'I wouldn't like to be within twenty-five yards of it!' It sounds so funny now, but the story is quite true, I assure you. Twenty-five yards! What chance against a German paratrooper? But then paratroopers had not been heard of.

After the probationary period of the L.D.V., Frankton Home Guard was formed around the summer of 1940, Mr. Walley, a local farmer, was made Lieutenant. There were three Sergeants, Tom Haynes, Dave Phillips and George Davies; two Corporals and the rest were Privates, in all about thirty men of all ages and sizes, who had known each other all their lives. They used to meet in the Parish Hall for rifle instruction, machine-gun instruction and to learn how to throw a handgrenade (when previously I would imagine that the majority of them had only used a catapult or thrown a stone at a rabbit).

I remember Dad telling me of the early days. Frankton Home Guard went for an hour's 'Square Bashing' at Park Hall Camp — a regular army barracks close by. One Sunday morning Mr. Berwick, the Stationmaster, insisted he could not go on parade without his walking stick, and I think my Dad and one or two others, who didn't have proper army caps, went on parade, some in bowlers and some in cloth caps and trilbys. The Sergeant Major, whose job it was to try and knock this Frankton Platoon into shape on that particular day, stopped after about a quarter of an hour. I think he was shattered when my Dad said: 'Don't you think we are a smart body of men?' The reply came: 'You bloody well are!' I don't think they ever went there again after that. I think the powers that be decided that as long as they could use a rifle or a shotgun, that would be enough for them to defend Frankton.

Sure enough, one night very soon afterwards, they thought the time had come for just that. I remember Mr. Walley knocking loudly on our door at the Perthy in the early hours of the morning and informing my Dad that they thought the invasion of England had started!

Whether Dad was still half asleep and not responding very well may have caused the remark: 'Wake up Joe, the buggers will be coming up the Brow before we are ready for them.' Dad got up in such a hurry that he put his trousers on back to front. However, we lads were woken and told to go around our little Perthy section knocking up the neighbourhood and telling them to assemble at the Smithy at once and to be prepared to fight.

The total assembly at the Smithy was about 10 men. Their weapons were two old American Ross rifles, 10 rounds of ammunition, one 12-bore shotgun with two cartridges, one four-ten shotgun that had been left out in the rain, with the inside of the barrel really rusty. One of the men was a complete stranger. It appears he had come for a few day's holiday to Brow Farm as he was a part-time

67

fireman in Liverpool and had been fighting fires for about ten nights on the run.

It did not take these men long to get ready for the battle they thought was soon to start. First they lit the two hurricane lamps that Dad had to light the Smithy. Then someone lit the Smithy fire; out came the old cast-iron kettle; a packet of tea, old tots, and a plank of wood was placed across the two anvils to form extra seating arrangements. The first brew-up was soon being drunk. The fact that sparks from the Smithy fire were lighting the outside of the Smithy did not enter their heads. My particular memory of that scene is of about ten or a dozen men who had their priorities right — having a cup of tea first. Hitler would have to wait for them. I often wonder with that scene still fresh in my mind, what a German paratrooper would have made of it if he had looked through the door. Who knows, perhaps he would have joined them and had a cup of Joe Strange's tea.

The Ridge Section, at the other end of the village, had orders to defend the road where three lanes converge. This was a particularly difficult part of our village to defend! Three roads and only about eight or nine men to defend them. Here too, a great tactical decision was taken. One lane was to be blocked with an old harvest wagon and both the other two could then be seen from the Dutch barn.

Two rifles and ten rounds of ammunition! Imagine them lying in wait for a German tank to come. Suddenly one of them jumped up and said: 'I've been thinking, some beggar might run into that harvest wagon and smash it up'. After a long discussion, they lit a spare hurricane lamp and hung it on the shafts of the wagon! Once again, I wonder what a German tank commander would have thought. He might have turned back, suspecting a secret weapon!

The top Frankton section were to defend the main road by the Parish Hall. They got their priorities right too! They got both the old coke stove and the oil lamps that hung over the billiard table in the Hall going. Blankets were found, and in no time at all, they had a rota, — two on duty outside to warn of the attacking German forces, the others allowed to stay in the warm and sleep on the billiards table.

When Doug Richardson's turn to go on patrol came, he suggested they turn the lights down low as he could see them from the road.

This they did, not aware what Doug was planning. Alf Colesby had a goat tethered in Miss King's garden and Doug decided to see how alert the others were. He sneaked up the garden, grabbed the goat by the collar and took him to the billards room door. Flinging the door open, he shoved the goat inside and shouted, 'Aye up, I've got a prisoner!' The goat went bounding around the room, bleating like mad, knocking chairs and men over in its mad scramble to escape. What a sight it must have been. It is a wonder someone was not shot, and I believe there was a rush for the one and only men's toilet.

The Germans did not invade and later on when you read my piece of poetry you will know the reason why.

Frankton Home Guard was now getting more organised. Three new lookout posts were made, one high in Frankton Church spire, another in a dug-out in the field on the top of the Brow with a large wire rope that could be stretched across to a post in the hedge on the opposite side of the main road, and the third in another dug-out in one of the Perthy fields. They made a ringed fortress around our little village!

The one in the church spire was, and still is a wooden platform reinforced by angle iron and bolted through the outlook windows threequarters of the way up the spire, reached by a thirty foot ladder off the belfry floor. It was quite a precarious job getting up to it and I believe on occasions there were one or two narrow squeaks when the odd Home Guard had been for a drink or two before ascending the ladder. Every night, two or three men of Frankton Home Guard manned this spot, watching for any parachutist landing. One can see for miles from this tower; I have been up there many times since and the view is quite breath-taking. This ladder is no longer there — only the platform remains as a permanent reminder to the villagers of the part Frankton Home Guard played in the defence of England.

One can smile about it now but at the time it seemed very important to the people of our little village. The other two look-outs have been filled in. I pass them by occasionally on my walks, and pause to think of some of the men who manned these sites, all having done a day's work before they went on night duty. Humble country characters doing what they thought was right. No questions were asked, no payment was expected.

One character I particularly remember was Mackie. At the outbreak of war he had a boat on the canal at Lower Frankton. He decided to dock the Duchess Countess on the side of the canal bank for the duration. Where he came from I do not know, only that he joined Frankton Home Guard and seemed quite happy to go on duty almost every night in the church spire. He was a stocky man who could quote Shakespeare extensively. How I wish now that I had the patience to listen to him. He certainly was a very educated man and must have had hundreds of stories to tell of a different kind of life to what I have known.

One night it was Frankton Home Guard's turn to stop cars on the canal bridge. Not many cars were allowed out at night, petrol was strictly rationed. One particular car had a couple of times previously failed to stop when challenged, swerving around the Home Guard Patrol. That night, they were ready for it or him. He came as usual, — same procedure. He would slow down a bit and then accelerate off again. But I'll bet he was not banking on what was about to happen; One of them, just as his tail light was disappearing around the corner, put a bullet through his back window, obviously not hitting him. The funny thing was, he was never seen on the main road again. He must have changed his route or ran out of petrol. I wonder which? How true the story is that they sent a Home Guard out on a push-bike to get his number I don't know.

One Sunday afternoon, in a big exercise, Frankton Home Guard was to defend the locks at Lower Frankton, and avoid capture from a platoon of regular soldiers from Park Hall Camp! Somehow or other the regulars got the Frankton platoon surrounded and their Sergeant Major came forward to claim: 'You've all been shot and platoon has captured Frankton Locks', 'Don't talk so bloody soft', said Lieutenant Walley, and gave Sergeant Major a thump with his rifle butt knocking him flying into the canal. He couldn't swim, and had to be unceremoniously dragged to the side — end of exercise! What the outcome was, I don't know, but there were no more sorties arranged between the army and Frankton Home Guard. What a blow it must have been to the man's pride and dignity; and I imagine a few of his own troops had a quiet smile. Heaven help 'em on parade the next morning!

Whether or not it was the same Sergeant Major who was giving lectures in Frankton Parish Hall, I don't know, but he asked the assembled platoon that if a German soldier appeared in that doorway right now 'What steps would you take?', and the answer came: 'Big buggers through the other door'.

On another night-parade in the Parish Hall the Home Guard was expecting an armoured car from Park Hall Camp to be demonstrated to them. A vehicle drew into the yard with a terrible roar. As they all trooped outside, they found it was Alf Colesby, an insurance collector, arriving home late. The silencer had fallen off his Morris-Eight car. Another false alarm!

As the war progressed and supplies were more plentiful, Frankton Home Guard became quite well equipped. A rifle each, a couple of sten-guns, a few handgrenades and a machine-gun. The older men were disbanded and were only to be called upon if the occasion arose. This left a much smaller platoon, much more effective in fire power and I am sure that if the need had arisen they would have given a good account of themselves. As I look back on those days how funny it all seems, but how serious it was then!

This happened to another Home Guard Platoon. I mention no names but the Sergeant-in-charge was showing village lads how to load and unload a rifle. In great detail he explained how serious and dangerous it was, and at the close said you should always 'fire' the empty rifle into the ground away from anyone to make sure no live round is left in the breach. This he did and shot straight through the frame of his bike which was leaning against the ditch bank! He quickly recovered explaining that was the point he was making, and how dangerous a loaded rifle could be. George Cleveley welded and repaired the frame of the bike for him.

When the war finished I, somehow or other, acquired a photograph of Frankton Home Guard. For many years it hung on my smithy door. One morning I found every face had been disfigured with a nail or sharp instrument. It was completely ruined. At the time, I was very upset, because I thought it was the only copy in being. I rounded up every youth and young man in the village and got them all in the smithy one night to try to find out whether any of them had done it, or whether they knew who had. I accused practically every one of them. Realising I was not getting anywhere with my questioning, I gave them a stern lecture and told them how

71

in later years the photograph might have an important place in the history of Frankton.

Suddenly, a youth said: 'I dunno think it is any of the village lads, Alfred, because I remember on the photo that my Dad had a hole in his head when I was going to school'. End of case!

When Frankton Home Guard disbanded, another bit of country history ended. This recitation altered by me to include the names of people from our village, is my tribute to:

FRANKTON HOME GUARD

The other day, just a bit since,
Two fellows sat both looking glum.
One was the great Adolf Hitler
T'other was Goering, his chum.

Now Adolf heard Goering was saying
'It's high time that thou made a move,
'Thou promised that thou'd invade England
'Our power to finally prove.'

'I've cleared the way with the Luftwaffe
'I've brought the R.A.F. down to the ground
'For each plane we 'av lost they 'av lost seven
'Or do they mean t'other way round?'

'On water there's nothing to stop thee
'Tho'rt Master of Sea thou knows that,
'So what in the world does't thou wait for?'
'Invade um I want a new hat!'
'Owd hard', said Hitler
'You am forgotten just one thing
Frankton Home Guard.'

Well at first owd Goering he looked puzzled
Then taking his coat by the 'em
And bursting out laughing right loudly, he said,
'You dunna mean to say yum frittened o' them?'

'Why, the'm only Lieut. Walley's army
'Instructed by Sgts. Davies and Haynes;
'They'm bow legged, knock-kneed and bandy',
'But', said Hitler 'by gum they got brains'.

'And there is one other thing to consider
'Which is the reason for most of me fears
'There is about thirty of 'em
'And everyone Volunteers'.

And if some of 'em are a bit wheezy,
And if some of 'em walk with a stick,
The more John Bull appears crippled
The harder the fool seems to kick.

In my opinion that piece of poetry sums it up. That is the reason Hitler did not invade England. Thanks to the many Home Guard Platoons of our country, but mainly to Frankton's. Surely they helped rewrite the history of the world.

When the Volunteer force (to stem the invasion!!!), was first formed, it was called officially, that is — Local Defence Volunteers. Unofficially it was known as 'Look, Duck and Vanish'. Rifles were broom handles, their uniform, an L.D.V. arm-band. No doubt Capt. Mainwaring would have been duly impressed.

In 1942 my old school teacher Clayton Jones, was put in charge of the newly-formed Criftins Army Cadets. Criftins is the next village to Frankton, and he asked some of his old pupils to join them. About four or five of us from Frankton did so, and every Wednesday night we had instruction on the use of different army equipment: We had a week-end camp at Boratten Hall, loaded up and taken there by Charlie Paddock in one of the waggons.

I was made up to Sergeant Major after about a month, I think because I was the oldest lad in the squad. We had a week's camp at Lythe Hill by Bayston Hill, in the first year and the following year at Church Stretton. It was good experience for us youngsters and to me a welcome change from being under horses all the while. I was never destined to go in the army, but I am sure that the training and companionship I found in the Cadets had I been called up would have stood me in good stead. I was not called up because the Authorities must have thought I was more useful to the War effort, helping my Dad to shoe horses and repair implements to produce more food. If I have any complaint to make about my life it is that I have a feeling that I missed out by not joining the forces.

I had no wish to take anyone's life, but when I hear my four brothers reminiscing of the many places they visited while on Army Service I am quite envious. I never even did any National Service, but that was due to the death of my Dad and my becoming Village Blacksmith.

Chapter 9

'Mother Was The Farmer — But A Mother First'

OCCASIONALLY my Dad used to go to Oswestry on a Wednesday with Wynne to take pigs, or perhaps a cow to market. He was no farmer; he would sooner shoe a horse than milk a cow any day, but would go to market whenever there was something to sell — perhaps it was the chance of a day out with Wynne.

Mother was the farmer, best in the Perthy set-up. Wynne once told me how one Tuesday, the day before piglets, born eight weeks earlier on our smallholding, were to be taken to market. Dad took Wynne to the sty to look them over.

'Joe, they am as nice a bunch of pigs as I've seen for a long time. They am a credit to you, you should be proud of them,' Wynne said, and my Dad's face lit up, all smiles.

Next day, they loaded the pigs into Wynne's lorry and while Dad went into the house to put on his clean overalls and to oil his workingboots with oil from his blacksmith's shop, Wynne remarked to Mother what nice pigs they were while she was making him his usual cup of tea. (She usually also gave him an ounce of twist tobacco as a tip).

Before she could answer, my Dad came out, ready for off in clean overalls, clean collar and stiff white front under his waistcoat. 'Do you know,' she said, 'yesterday was the first time he saw those piglets in the eight weeks of their lives!'

She had to give up retailing milk halfway through the war. Not because it did not pay — it never had anyhow — and not because of its quality, that was tip top (except when the Anker's girl watered it down by drinking half the can and topping it up with well water).

No, the reason was more complicated. As a retailer, you had to obtain coupons from customers for the amount of milk they were entitled to have, using those same coupons in turn to acquire your corn requirements. Coupons and Mother never got on together — she'd always give a pint and a half — or even a quart — if there were babies in the house, when a pint should have been delivered.

Hitler could not change her ways, but the consequence was that month by month her entitlement of corn grew smaller and smaller. In the end, of course, it had to stop, but in truth it was the children of Perthy who were the real sufferers. One can only hope that other children received what they were missing as a result and that the milk was not flushed down a drain somewhere as surplus to requirements. Mother could not make anything of those damned coupons. 'Who's having the corn, our corn, if we're not,' she would ask. She just could not comprehend the significance of U-Boats and convoys.

To get one's correct share of feeding stuffs for pigs, they started 'Pig Clubs' in each area. I must confess, I never understood their purpose. (They all seemed to meet in pubs). For Ellesmere and district, the man who ran it, Bill Tims, used to have the garage, with his brother Bert, next to Dave Evans' yard, where the Fire Engine was kept. How he came to be mixed up with pigs I don't know. Dad and I couldn't help thinking that if Mother had been dealing in bacon instead of pigs, the same would have been the result as with the pints of milk.

A rather large family was living on the Perthy soon after the outbreak of war. Another baby had just arrived making, I believe, double figures. A village girl from a cottage near the Smithy asked her Mother if she could go to see the new arrival. 'No,' had been the first answer, but she persisted. 'Oh, go on Mam, I only want to go for a minute or so to see the new baby.' 'Oh alright,' relented her Mother, 'But don't you stop very long. The Mother of the new baby will be tired and won't want to be mithered with someone else's children.'

My Mother was outside when the girl came along, unable to contain her excitement. 'Can you carry a basket, Mary?' Mother asked. 'Course I can, Mrs. Strange.' Within two minutes Mother had gone inside and was out again, with a basketful — eggs, buns, fruit and butter. The girl did not stay very long and when she came back with the basket she said to my Mother: 'Oh Mrs. Strange, the new baby is lovely.' 'What did the baby's Mother say to you?' Mother asked. 'Oh not much,' was the reply. 'She was in bed, and too busy skinning a rabbit for dinner.' That was very acceptable knowing that mother.

Disposable nappies? Health Visitors? they were a world away. Andrew Baird used to travel round the various villages as a salesman for Baird's, the Gentlemen's Outfitters in Oswald Street, Oswestry, opposite the Old Railway Station. Like all travellers he used to have a cup of tea at the Perthy, arriving on his pushbike from Oswestry. Mother paid so much a week for trousers or jackets for us lads. Both he and Dad smoked pipes, and often tried to cadge pipefuls off each other, when they had an ounce or so in hand. Dad smoked *Tom Moody*, Mr. Baird *Virginia*, I think. He never wore shoes, always boots, and his bicycle clips looked ever so odd so high on his legs.

Mother told me one night, just after the end of the war, to go to Mr. Baird's house in Oswestry — he had something for me. I arrived at his house around 7 p.m. and I thought he seemed rather subdued. 'Try this overcoat on, Alf,' he said. I did so. It fitted me very well.

'Do you like it?' he said. 'Yes,' I replied, and was just about to add: 'We can't afford to buy it,' when he said: 'There, I'm giving you that as a present.' I was dumbfounded. A practically new best overcoat, GIVEN to me, just like that! I would be a toff, I thought, and the envy of all the village lads. Thanking him very much, I came home to Frankton, where Mother asked: 'What did Mr. Baird want?' I told her.

The coat had belonged to his son Don who had been killed in the war. I treasured it, and still have it 40-odd years later, a little thread-bare now, as it was used for every day in the bad winters of 1963 and 1979. When he gave it to me I did not realise what a traumatic

77

time it was for him. Though the war was over, families like Andrew Baird's were beginning to come to terms with the sad fact their son or daughter would not be returning.

Andrew Baird's story shows another aspect of life in a rural community after the war. He lost two sons, Don and Etrick. The enormity of it all only hits you when you have children and grandchildren of your own.

I have in my Smithy still, a pewter urn. How to value it I don't know, but it holds a special place in my memories for Mother used to hide five or six ounces of tobacco in it. During the war, as I have mentioned before, tobacco was hard to get and as Dad could easily get through an ounce a day it was essential for her to keep a few in reserve, if she wanted to keep him in a good mood. Many times at breakfast I have heard Dad saying: 'Well Em. (he always called her Em.) 'Well Em.,' he would say, 'I have only got one pipe of tobacco to last the day.' Mother would banter a bit and say: 'Well it's no good asking me for any, I canna keep up with yu and yur blooming 'bacca.' Later on when Mother was out in the farmyard, Dad, who knew Mother had some 'bacca somewhere, would search everywhere in the house and in the pantry.

Suddenly on that particular day he found this pewter jar, in it was about four or five ounces, *John Peel, Tom Moody, Thick Twist,* and all sorts. Not satisfied with just taking one ounce, he was sorting them out, deciding which one to take when Mother caught him. 'Well you found it,' said she.

There was no row, — that's the way it was with them, trust, respect and love for one another. Every time I handle that pewter urn the memory of the tobacco day comes back to me. And one of the pleasant pictures and memories is that of seeing Dad going across to the smithy with a pipe full of freshly lit tobacco, like the *Queen Mary* leaving Liverpool. On reflection though, it was one of the few pleasures that the average country working man had, a pipe of tobacco and a pint of beer — not much by today's standard.

My Mother was not very well one day. This meant that Frank and I had to get meals ready for Dad. We asked Mother, who was in bed, whether she wanted anything to eat, she said she did not feel like anything, only a cup of tea. However, Frank decided to cut her a cheese buttie, and put three or four pickled onions on the plate.

What an inviting and tasty meal, pickle onions and cheese butties, for someone who could manage just a cup of tea! Three parts of the way upstairs the pickle onions rolled off the plate, and Mother said she heard them bouncing down the stairs. Frank placed the plate on the top step leading to the bedroom and went down to pick them up. He put them back on the plate and took them into the bedroom for Mother. There was no carpet on our stairs in those days, that's how Mother could hear them (I don't know if she felt better or worse for the pickles.)

A little home-made poetry:

WHEN MOTHER OR DAD IS SICK

When me Dad is sick he is scared to death,
And Mother and us just owds our breath,
He crawls to bed, he puffs, he grunts,
And does all kinds of crazy stunts.
He wants the Doctor mighty quick,
For when me Dad's ill he is awful sick.

Now when me Mother is sick, she pegs away,
Quiet though, not much to say,
She goes right on a-doing things,
And sometimes laughs and even sings,
She says she doesn't feel 'extra well,'
It's just a kind of a spell,
She will be alright tomorrow,
A good night's rest will be her cure.

Me Dad, he sniffs and makes a kick,
He says 'Women folk are always sick',
Me Mother smiles, lets on she is glad,
When me Mother's sick, it tinna half so bad.

I have lost count of the times that I recited that poem over the years at concerts and Chapel Do's. Only last year I recited it as a request in our top Chapel. The words ring true to me, to the present day.

This next story is about hay harvest, but ends up by being a story of Mother. The sun was shining on a beautiful June day in 1950. The only thing wrong was that I was on my own, up to me neck with work at the Smithy; every farmer seemed to have something he wanted mended, hay turner, mowing machines, and all forms of agriculture implements converted from horse-drawn to tractor-driven (machines spud picking, that were never designed to do so). Breakdowns were frequent, bringing increased work for the village blacksmith. A horse stops if he feels something wrong, a tractor keeps on going. (It was always desperately busy in a smithy when the hay harvesting got under way.)

The day in question was when I had borrowed my Uncle Jack's pony to turn our six acres of hay. The pony had been harnessed to the hay turner since ten o'clock in the morning, and it was now half-past two, and I still had not been able to get to the hayfield, missing the best of the hot sun. At last about three o'clock I was able to start for the field, having gone without my dinner as well.

About a hundred yards up the road I met Mrs. Hilda Price hurrying along. She stopped me. She was quite out of breath. 'Please ring the Doctor for Mrs. Phillips. She is not at all well.'

'I can't stop,' I said, 'My house door is unlocked, go and ring the Doctor yourself.'

'I don't know how to use the telephone,' she said, which was quite true.

'All you have to do is to lift the 'phone, wait until a voice says to you, "what number do you want"?' I said. 'Then you say that you want putting through to the Ellesmere Doctor, which Mrs. Humphreys in the telephone exchange will do for you quite easily.'

I realised that Mrs. Price was not going to be able to use the 'phone as she was too upset and distraught in her concern for Mrs. Phillips. I turned the pony round in the road and went back to the Smithy, tying the pony up to the old oak tree. By this time I was getting a bit short tempered. I got through to the Doctor, explained the message that I had for him. Whether my tone of voice upset him, I don't know but his reply was: 'Have you read your medical card?'

'What the hell's that got to do with the message?' I asked.

'Well,' he said, 'If you read your medical card it says "ring before 10 o'clock in a morning if you want a Doctor to visit you that same day!"'

I did not try to argue with him. I just repeated the message to him loud and clear and finished by saying, 'It's up to you whether you come out or not, I have got something better to do than stand here holding this 'phone.' and put the telephone down.

Mother was sitting in his surgery while this was going on, unknown to me. The Doctor remarked to her 'That was some insulting young man from the Perthy on the 'phone.'

I saw Mother later in the week and told her the full story leading up to what the Doctor had said which had provoked my remarks to him. She was going to visit him again the following week, so I said: 'You can tell him that he is not the only one who is busy.' I knew she would tell the Doctor.

She started: 'Doctor, you know that "insulting young man" a week ago, was one of my *five* sons. No son of mine has ever been insulting to anyone without just cause. Doctors are not the only people pushed for time.'

I'm telling this story to show that it pays to make sure that you get your facts right, and try to put yourself in the other person's shoes in any argument. It shows I could depend on Mother backing up one of her sons — when he was in the right (but not otherwise).

Chapter 10

'Last of the 2,000 Dark Nights'

THE war was coming to its end in Europe; the D-Day landing had come in the previous June. I never went into the Army, I am not qualified to write about that. I try to write about what happened in Frankton, the last thing that this is, is a 'war book'.

Letters were still arriving from my three brothers. Tom was in the invasion of Normandy, Bill was in the Middle East and Jack was in Burma with 'Wingate's Chindits' getting ready to invade Japan. In Frankton we had formed a 'Welcome Home Fund' for village lads when they came back to 'Civvy Street'. It was to be a big celebration on a par with the Coronation or Jubilee Celebrations. Dad, I remember, said he would roll a barrel of beer up the middle of the hall and tap it on stage. Woe betide any trustees who tried to stop him, though beer was not allowed in the Parish Hall. I cannot recall whether he did so, but I do remember that beer was drunk in the hall on many occasions at the end of the war at different dances and 'do's'.

In an earlier chapter I mentioned the last important run of our lorry-cum-car. It was on 8th May, 1945, you will remember the date.

First I must tell of the night Ellesmere Young Farmers were challenged to a football match by Hodnet Young Farmers. The match was to be played at Hodnet, a village beyond Hawkestone

Park, 20 miles away. I was asked to play for Ellesmere at centre forward. Harry Benson, whose father farmed at Bagley, asked me to play. I had known Harry casually for a few years but not as a footballer. Our team were all Young Farmers from Ellesmere and after I asked my Father for the night off and got permission, Harry said: 'Oh, there's a bet on the game, we're playing for a pound a man.' (Even in those days 'Young Farmers' were the affluent society, £1 then would be equal to £30 today.) 'A pound a man', I thought. I did not see that in a month's wages working for my Dad. I dare not ask him for it. He would have told me to go and get my head seen to, and find something better to do with his money. But I had already said 'yes' and pride would not let me pull out. I managed to keep in my Mother's good books and persuaded her to lend me a pound. I promised to pay it back. How, I hadn't the foggiest, if we didn't win. I didn't tell her what it was for, only that I was playing football and needed it to go. John Dutton from a nearby farm was to pick me up at about 5.30 p.m. and we were to meet at Bagley Hall Farm and go in convoy (Army terms catching up on me) from there. John brought his mother with him, his brother Dick and sister Margaret. Dick Dutton, I remember, on sick leave from the Army, wore a uniform of light blue. The car was a maroon Hillman Minx No. FNU 12. A good car, but it had no spare wheel but more about that later.

Arriving at Bagley, I was transferred to Harry Benson's car, an Austin-Ten straight back. Away we went with a crashing of gears in a cloud of smoke. I think there were about six of us in this car, all players. Going through one village, we saw a flock of chickens crossing the road. I thought 'slow down Harry, you'll run over some of them'. He did just the opposite, opening the throttle a bit more, scattering the hens in all directions. Someone looked through the back and said: 'I think you got two and winged two more Harry.' We went on our way laughing eventually arriving at Hodnet at Whiston's Farm House where we were to meet and change for the match. Imagine a crowd of Young Farmers descending on you, all wanting to change at the same time.

Mrs. Whiston put up with us and off we went down to the football field. Petrol was rationed and only essential journeys were allowed but someone at Hodnet had had the bright idea of inviting the local

Bobby, Bill Hopkins, to be referee. Money for the side bets had been collected by him and placed in his helmet. £22 was a small fortune to us, at least to me, in those days.

At last the game got underway and immediately I had a sinking feeling the Hodnet side was far too good for us. We were soon two goals down, and Dennis Hockenhull, one of our players, had never played football, only rugby. I can see him now! A Hodnet player pushed the ball past him, who had a great shock, for Dennis made a flying rugby tackle good enough to grace an international.

They scored five goals to our two; I scored both our goals.

As the policeman referee blew for time, there was an announcement that the war was over! ! ! Peace was declared! The £22 was placed over the Bar at the ground and drinks were flowing like water from a tap. Someone announced a dance had been arranged at the Bear Hotel.

After we finished drinking at the club we trooped off to the Bear. More beer was bought there, I presume with the rest of the money from the bets. I know that I had no money with me. What time we left Hodnet I don't know, but I remember arriving back to Cockshutt with the Dicken lads whose Dad kept the Red Lion. We opened up there. More drinks. Breathalyser, what was that?

We then went on to Tom Lindop's home at the Fearny. We suddenly remembered we had left Mrs. Dutton and Margaret, her daughter there. Tom Lindop, John Dutton and myself were by this time feeling the pressure of such a hectic evening; we had no idea of the time. Mrs. Dutton, who was not very well at the time, had gone to lie down and had to be woken up. I remember the dressing down she gave us three, and her low opinion of the youth of the day! Not daring to answer back, we stood quite sheepish with the effects of the beer beginning to wear off. Eventually, we got into her car with another six miles to go. Margaret was driving, but worse was to happen yet. Coming into Tetchill, bang went a tyre. Remember, it was wartime, only four tyres on the car. Mrs. Dutton started another lecture, but I decided not to listen, and said: 'I'll run home to the Perthy and get our old car-cum-lorry out to fetch you.'

There was a light on at our house when I arrived. I walked in and Mother was in the kitchen — she had just got up. It was about

5.30 a.m. Not giving her a chance to start a lecture, I explained what had happened and asked her if she knew the war was over. She said she did, but another one would start when I got back home. I went to pick up Mrs. Dutton, Margaret and John. Loading Mrs. Dutton in the front, John and Margaret got on to the back of the lorry-cum-car. I got them home safely, arriving back just in time for breakfast and to start to milk our few cows. Mother had cooled down by the time we had milked and as we listened to the early morning news on our old battery wireless set, she suddenly realised the war was over and that her sons would soon be returning to the fold. Her family would be complete again for the first time in six years. We did not do much work that day, Thank God. People kept calling at the Perthy and the whole village was in a state of excitement as the news started to dawn on our small community. Little did I realise then that life would never be the same again.

A message came through that there would be a dance at Hordley Parish Hall that night, and a gang of us went on our bikes to The Fox at Bagley for more celebrations before going to the dance. At about 10 p.m., Dad, Ern Edwards and Edwin Peever arrived, having called at The Fox themselves, and having earlier been to Tom Williams, the T. C. Price driver's house for cowhorns to place on our bellows pole. They had the horns sticking out of their coat pockets and it is not hard to imagine the merriment those cowhorns caused!

I offered to get their tea, which then cost about 2d a cup. Dad gave me two bob to pay for them. When I offered him the change, he said: 'You can keep it'. 1s. 6d was worth a lot to me then.

For the record, I think the Hodnet team that night before, was: Tim and Peter Brookshaw (Tim later became a jockey and came second in the Grand National on Wynborough), John and Frank Apperley (Frank was Captain of Hawkestone Golf Club in 1984/85 and in the 1960s was Captain of Shropshire Cricket Club), Roy, Tom and Val Whiston, Ron Taylor (Captain of Hawkestone now), Don Morgan, Bill France and Arthur Jones. (The Whiston brothers are well-known racehorse trainers).

The Ellesmere teams were:

George Lea, Harry Benson, John Benson, John Dutton, Norman Birch, Alf Hulme, Tom Nicholas, Dennis Hockenhull, Tom Lindop,

Tom Downing, Bill Ralphs, John Elder and Alf Strange. Our linesman was Albert Gregory and that's after two nights of hard drinking. Their chief supporter deserves a mention, Tom Morgan. A return match was fiixed for a later date at Cockshutt and we lost that as well! What the stakes were I don't know, perhaps we had learnt our lesson.

That same evening a race had been arranged between Frank Apperley and George Lea, over 100 yards. I remember it was carrying a bit of money. Frank Apperley, who won, could do 100 yards in 10.4 seconds, quite quick for a lad in those days. He had proper running shoes with spikes and somebody remarked that they hoped he would not be allowed to play football in them! So ended 2,000 nights of blackout.

Some of the players have passed on to pastures new. Some of us are still left with aches and pains but still enjoying our pint, or, in most cases, a drop of Scotch. As I sit here writing, memories of those two nights come flooding back to me. The happiness and comradeship will never return, but all who took part in them look back with happy memories.

When you young 'uns look at some of us 'owd 'uns, we could run a bit, play football a bit, and cricket, even if we hadn't got all the gear that you have today. The motto was 'never mind the result, but play the game in a true sporting manner'. I must stop preaching or the readers will fall asleep.

During the war, Frankton people formed a 'Welcome Home Fund' so that when the lads came home a real welcome would await them. A big party was to be arranged in the Parish Hall, like almost all villages and streets in towns. Whist drives, dances, and concerts were held. It was like the parish hall building fund raising of twenty years earlier.

Frankton folk went through the war much the same as most other villages. I remember one old lady saying when she heard on the wireless that Tito of Yugoslavia was leading the guerillas into action against the German army, that although she hated the Germans she did not believe in letting the 'gorillas' loose on the German soldiers! A new word she did not know what it meant. Mopping up operations had many old village folk thinking it must be dirty 'over there'.

During the war there was a Woman's Land Army Camp at

Queensbridge, Nr. Overton. Many of the girls married local lads, but one nearly didn't. The wedding was to take place at the girl's home town, Manchester. Ethel was to marry Jack, who lived and worked on a local farm at Lower Ridge. All his mates from Frankton were invited to the wedding. Tom Hyde's bus was hired to take us there, driven by Jack Reeves. The war had just ended — hence the private bus, by special authority, it was 26th July, 1946.

We arrived at a pub in Manchester; first priority was a drink after hours stuck in the bus, and two or three pints later we all boarded again to go to the Church. If we had known what the next two hours held, we would not have had so much to drink. We country lads crowded into the Church on time, but for an hour or so there was no sign of the bride. We were all feeling rather uncomfortable, crossing and uncrossing our legs. The parson was also getting very edgy and the other guests as well. There had been a mix-up between wedding cars: when someone went outside to find the cause of the delay (or, who knows, for other reasons?), it was to find that the driver of the wedding car had made a mistake. He thought someone else had brought the bride and was waiting outside the Church to take the couple to the reception. You can't have a wedding without the bride, who through no fault of her own had not been collected to be at the Church. She eventually arrived well over an hour late and the marriage took place.

After a good spread had been tucked away, it was time to get back on Hyde's bus. All twenty of us country lads, remember we'd had plenty to drink before the wedding — and our fair share at the reception — lined up to wish the couple 'all the best'. Then each and every one of us, claimed a kiss, — a real smacker, from all the bridesmaids. They were flabbergasted, saying: 'I didn't know country lads had it in them'. What a cheek, I bet we Welsh Frankton lads could have shown city slickers a thing or two.

They have lived in Criftins all their married life and now forty years later have a son and daughter-in-law, and two grandsons who make their home in *the* village of Welsh Frankton — they must have some good sense, in spite of the start.

Jack Davies, my Aunty Sally's son from Wallasey, and our cousin, had been a Prisoner of War in Japanese hands since the fall of Singapore in 1942 until his release in early 1946. He came to spend a

87

few days with us at the Perthy. He was never very robust so you can imagine what he looked like after four years imprisoned. He borrowed my Dad's 12-bore gun to shoot at rabbits down our big field and round Hardwick Pool.

George Pyke, the Estate Keeper, came tearing into our shop next day. He said to my Dad: 'Joe, who was that shooting down by the pool yesterday?' 'Oh, a nephew of mine from Wallasey,' said Dad. 'Well, you tell him Joe, that he can't go shooting again down by the Pool.' 'He's in the house,' said Dad, 'You go and tell him yourself, George. Before you go I want to tell you the lad has been a Prisoner of War in Japanese hands for the last four years.'

George hesitated a moment then, with a twinkle in his eye, said: 'Forget I called Joe, let the lad go where he wants.' Another true country story and an example of the respect village people had for one another in those days.

All our lads came back, — save the two whom I mentioned, Raymond Jones and Geoff James.

Chapter 11

'Village Charity With A Capital C'

THERE was a charity left to the village of the Perthy. Every Christmas, Captain Owen from the Groves at Criftins brought it round for my Dad to deliver to the poorer families. £5/11/11d. it was, in total, no more; no less. At one time it would go to eleven families. 10/- each, to ten houses and 11s. 11d. to the other house. It was left to Dad, when someone who had been receiving it died off, to nominate another family. As the years went by, 10/- bought less, (at one time it would buy 5 or 6 cwt. of coal, or 30 loaves). Dad used to arrange it so that eventually five families received £1 which was the case until recently. I used to deliver it every Christmas. Harold Evison brought it instead of Captain Owen. A pound buys about two loaves, a few lumps of coal or some nutty slack. It was only an old tradition I hoped would keep going, as once it stops that will be it. Why it was no more, due to inflation, I don't know. If you were entitled to 10/- in the thirties, surely it must be worth pounds now.

One old boy who used to receive this ten 'bob' was an ex-soldier. When he received it — to say it went on food or coal would be a little way from the truth. You would knock on his door and he would shout 'come in'. He was the spitting image of Lord Kitchener. His house was ramshackle with newspapers in some windows that had not seen glass for many years. I went in, he was in his armchair and the cat was on the rug in front of what bit of fire he had. I made a noise with my mouth: the cat took one leap straight through the newspaper in the window and out, up the garden. He said: 'I wonder what the hell's got into her.' I could hardly stop myself from laughing. Stupid little anecdotes, but oh, how they reek of country life.

Another old lad who received 10/- lived in a little cottage about 200 yards down the field, not far from Frankton Station. Taking his required two of us. He seemed to know when to expect the ten shillings, Christmas week as a rule. If it was given to him, he would be away on the twenty-to-twelve train to Ellesmere for a few drinks. Mother's plan was: one of us walked past his cottage making sure he had been seen, then the other one, who would keep out of sight the other side of the cottage, while the other kept him talking, would then deliver the 10/- charity to his wife, at the back door. A tactical move.

I wrote earlier that I had hoped this village tradition would carry on until my time was over. I have received a letter this morning from the powers that be. It has been decided that the Frankton Five Pound should go into a General fund, as it is only through my efforts that Frankton for the last five years has still had the charity, other villages lost theirs in 1980. How sad it is another country village tradition allowed to fade and die. I am told it is progress. I doubt it.

It has at least given me, for the last fifty odd years or so, much pleasure talking to pensioners and the like who received the Frankton charity. You learnt more about village life and history in a five minute chat than you could out of half a dozen books. The University of life, it's called.

Another old man used to get his bike out as soon as he got his money, to cycle at top speed to Oswestry, get drunk and cycle unsteadily back again.

It was in December 1985, I had the letter from Ellesmere Charities, signed by the Chairman and the Secretary, announcing it had been decided the local villages would no longer receive their annual cash. On what authority the Trustees reached this decision is not known by me. If it were not for the cost I would pursue this matter with the Charity Commission.

It is another instance of central bureaucracy killing off village life, a process which began when village schools were closed, and has been responsible for much of the hooliganism, and making it difficult to tell junior masters from senior lads. I know of an ex-councillor, who posed a question to a higher Council Official, — 'What are you going to do with the people already living in this hamlet?, Shoot them?' (It wasn't Welsh Frankton, Welsh Frankton is a village not a hamlet.)

One evening, about 10 o'clock, a knock at the door was answered by my Dad. It was George Antonio, the Stoke City football player, who played inside right to Stanley Matthews (now 'Sir') at that time. He had another Stoke City professional with him. (Later he came to give Frankton a coaching lesson). He had run out of petrol, just by our Lane end. Dad was all helpful. 'You're in luck, George, I've got two gallons in the shop.'

Out he went into the shop, got the old two gallon petrol tin, and lost no time walking down the lane to the stranded car. He had the good sense to take a funnel with him. I had been up at Tom Speke's when George called.

When I got in I said to Mother: 'Where's me Dad?' She told all about the charitable act. 'Good Lord,' I exclaimed, 'That inna petrol, it's water.' I raced down the lane, just in time to see Dad empty the last of the tin into the petrol tank!! Of course the vehicle wouldn't budge a yard. George and his mate had a six mile walk to Oswestry that night. Of course, I copped it. Somebody had to.

Chapter 12

' Four Funerals In Four Weeks '

AFTER he retired, Tommy Jones of No. 10 Higher Perthy used to go and help Tom Payne two days a week. I can hear him now going past the smithy, because he always wore clogs. He himself had about three acres of land, two cows, calves and a pig or two. Why I am writing about the lives and times of these two men, is that they died as did my Dad, within a short time of one another. All three lived within a few yards of each other, all were connected with the land, and all were respected village characters.

Tommy Jones was the first to die in August 1947, his daughter Hilda came to ask my Dad to be a bearer at his funeral. He had gone for a few days' holiday (I think his one and only holiday), to Fred Grundy's at Liverpool. We decided not to send a message to Liverpool, but rather I took his place, my first duty as bearer in senior company. I had served as bearer for a couple of school children, but it certainly was an honour to be asked to do so for a senior citizen.

There were many people about when I arrived at Mrs. Jones' house. Little did I think I was going to be involved in an incident. The hearse had arrived, — Lloyds of Oswestry, driven by Mr. Lloyd, senior. While waiting I leaned against the front mudguard of this immaculate polished hearse, Mr. Lloyd sharply told me: 'Canna you find somewhere else to lean on, I've spent all morning polishing it up.' 'Sorry' I said feeling uncomfortable, and completely out of place due to my youth.

After I had re-gained my composure and trying to bring a little relief to the occasion, I said: 'I'll tell my Dad about you shouting at me.' 'Oh! and who be your Dad?' was his reply. 'Joe Strange,' I said. 'Another thing,' I said, 'they would have a job to hide you in the cupboard at Vernons, the Grange.' 'What do you know about that?' he said. 'Oh me Mother has told me a lot of country tales like that' I said.

Many years earlier, well before the 1914-1918 war, and before my Mother and Dad were married in 1911, Mother was in service at Sampsons The Wood, Lower Frankton. Some evenings she, with Joe, then her boyfriend, would go up to the Grange, the evenings the Vernons were going out. Mother was friendly with one of the girls who worked at the Grange, and this night in question, the Vernons had gone out and the servant girl decided to invite one or two other lads and girls in to supper. Among them were George Lloyd, of Lloyds buses, Dad and Mother. The party was in full swing when they heard the Vernons returning.

They pushed the lads into the big kitchen cupboard; hurried around to clear the table, and when the Vernons entered they found only Mother and the other girl in the kitchen. Mother was accepted as a friend of the other girl. How long Dad and George were in the cupboard I don't know, but we both agreed that funeral day, Mr. Lloyd and me, that they would have had a job to put him in the cupboard then, because the day of Tommy Jones' funeral he would be about eighteen stone. As I bade him goodbye he said to me: 'Remember me to Joe, your Dad.' Little did I think that both he and Dad would be dead within a month.

Three weeks later Mr. Lloyd got up out of his sick bed to attend Dad's funeral and a week or so later he himself died. A few days later Tom Payne passed away: who would have credited it, the four men, all connected with village life would pass away almost together. But life had to go on; they were all missed very much in their various homes. Mother missed two good neighbouring small-holders, who would surely have been a great help and comfort to her in her own bereavement. The old country saying of the churchyard is that it is full of indispensable people.

Funerals remind me of the Rev. Victor McMunn, our C. of E. Vicar. He was a very cheerful robust chap who had an infectious laugh. An ex-naval man, I am told he once said that with his naval telescope, from the top of the Brow Bank, he could see the ships on the Mersey. He was also a very generous man, and many parcels of groceries he left on the doorsteps of older villagers, and some poorer families in our village. He was a very learned man, and he was translating the Bible into a language that was only known to a nearly extinct tribe. He lived in the Vicarage, at the top end of the village, by the Church. He never married but had Mr. and Mrs. Jim Brayne to look after him. Mr. Brayne was also Sexton and used to dig the graves in our churchyard. I remember once in class at Frankton School one village lad said to me: 'I wonder who will dig Mr. Brayne's grave.'

In later years Mr. McMunn was a bit forgetful and one day got on the train at Ellesmere to attend a meeting at Chester. He fell asleep on the train and arrived at Birkenhead, and wasn't too clear to the police as to what he was doing there. However, after a lot of questioning the police put him back on the train to Frankton. Maybe they thought he was a spy because he dressed a little bit eccentric, with, I seem to remember, a suit that was about two sizes too big for him.

A funeral in his day was quite a big occasion, he would go to the house, have a short prayer, maybe a hymn or a lesson, and then a full funeral service at the Church. As he got older he had to be picked up by car and taken to the different houses. One day it fell to me to pick him up and take him to a house down Lower Perthy for the funeral of Mrs. Matthew Jones (a sad day that was, she was only 43 years of age and left a baby daughter, Janet, and three other children, Lucy, Beryl and a son Maurice).

I picked the Vicar up, dressed in his Cassock and Surplice, — the lot. Why he got into the back seat of my four-door Morris-Eight, I don't know. The pre-war Morris was a very small car, and the back door opening was much smaller than the front, and also narrower at the bottom than at the top.

Arriving at the house which was across a small field, I went to open the back door to let the Vicar out. As he rose from the back seat, his legs gave way and there he was wedged in the doorway of

94

my car. I tried to pull him on my own. He found that quite amusing and started to chuckle. The more he chuckled the farther down he went to the floor of the car. I started to get a bit panicky; I went to try to find Eric Jones, the undertaker, he met me by the house door: 'Where have you been', he said 'and where's the Parson?' 'I've got him stuck in the back of me car, come and give us a lift.'

By this time all you could see of the Vicar were two legs protruding out of the door, the rest of his body was well and truly fast. Eric got in through the other back door and managed to get his hands under his armpits, I, by this time, had got hold of his hands and with a couple of heaves and a snatch, the Vicar shot out of the back door like a cork out of a bottle.

We tidied him up a bit and he went into the house to take the Service. After the Church Service I took him back to the Vicarage; he thanked me and said: 'Alf, I thought at one time I would have had to take the Service out of the back of your car.' On reflection, he could have been badly hurt; what would have happened then I don't know. I am sure that I would not have been the most popular character in the village.

Mr. McMunn died in 1950 and is buried in Welsh Frankton Churchyard where he himself had taken many funerals.

Chapter 13

' I Become A Blacksmith '

THE death of my Father, quite suddenly on a September evening, came as a terrific shock to me and my four brothers. I can remember as clearly as if it happened yesterday. It was my Mother's 61st birthday. We had had a fairly busy day in the blacksmith shop, shoeing a couple or three horses, making stays for a cart shaft for Mrs. Sampson, and brackets to hold a battery on Joe Clay's car. We had milked our few cows and had a little bit of a special tea (a tin of peaches). If my memory serves me right, by this time it would be about 7 o'clock.

Jack and I were the only brothers at home at that time. Tom and Bill were away and married and Frank was doing his National Service in the Army at Catterick, in Yorkshire. Jack and I had gone for a walk round the fields with the gun to try and get a rabbit for next day's dinner. We arrived back at about 9 o'clock, Mother had boiled onions for supper with fresh farm butter and home-made bread. The four of us ate, and Jack and I went to bed at about quarter to ten, Dad and Mother soon afterwards.

Only about a quarter of an hour later we heard Dad going down the stairs. A few minutes later, my Mother came into our bedroom to tell us to get up. We did so in double quick time.

Dad was outside in the yard at the Perthy, leaning over the railings trying hard to get his breath. I heard him saying to tell the doctor he could not get his breath. We had no telephone in those days. I got our old Morris out and went as fast as I could for Dr. Rogers who lived at the top of St. John's Hill in Ellesmere. Straight up the High Street I went, which was a one-way street. The Doctor answered the door. I explained quickly the position. He said: 'I'll follow you out straight away'.

I came straight back home to be met by Jack at the gate telling me it was all over, that my Dad had died before I had got to the bottom of the Brow Bank. Just as I left, he stood up, shook Jack's hand and said: 'Look after your Mother, put his arms around her and gave her a kiss. 'Goodbye old girl'. And those were the last words he said. Then, he sank to the ground and passed away. What a man!

But what lovely way to go. I little realised then what a change was to come over my life. Neighbours appeared from everywhere. Mrs. Butler arrived, took charge as she had done many times before when death came to other houses on the Perthy. She was the one who laid out the bodies. She was always present at births in the village, — and the deaths. What a comforting lady she was!

The next four days seemed an eternity. Then came the day of the funeral. Frankton Chapel was full to over-flowing with people standing about three deep on the main road all the way down to the churchyard. 136 wreaths were laid out over the grave. I believe it was the largest turnout to a funeral that Frankton people had ever witnessed. Eric Jones told me it was certainly the biggest he had ever undertaken.

When I look back and think of all the friends and customers he had over the forty-odd years as village blacksmith, it was no surprise, really. It was a send-off fit for a king. The funeral was on the Monday. I did not realise it then but I was now the village blacksmith, at the ripe old age of 21. I think that if I had known of the trials and tribulations and the heartaches that were to follow in the next few months and years I would have had second thoughts. To follow a master craftsman, who knew his job and commanded respect from every walk of life, from the landed gentry to the man in the street, is not an easy task.

On the Tuesday morning I looked around the Smithy, — my Smithy. My eyes fell on the anvil, I couldn't help thinking: 'That's

97

the same blooming anvil that Granny Strange sat on and scorched her bloomers.' Still full of grief, I couldn't help but raise a smile and a chuckle thinking about the old woman blacksmith. She may not have been the first woman blacksmith, but I dare bet she was the first to have three smithies, not to mention the anvil episode.

People can be cruelly forthright. One farmer, a few weeks after I started on my own, said: 'You'll never be half the man your Dad was!' I remember replying that if I could only be half as good I would reckon that to be a pretty good standard to achieve. Some customers left to get their work done elsewhere. 'There is no sentiment in business. Fight your own battles now lad, get stuck in and stand on your own two feet,' Mother told me. Sometimes people who you thought were your friends let you down and had work done elsewhere. Somewhere you found that you were shoeing their rough and unruly horses and another blacksmith shoeing their quiet ones. But thank goodness, all farmers were not like that. As in all life, farmers come good, bad, and in between.

One story now that is still fresh in my memory concerning an old man whose name was Bill Allman. He had a pony which we used to shoe. He was one of my first customers after I had started on my own. He came to the smithy one day and he said to me: 'Blacksmith, will you shoe my pony?' (He always called me 'Blacksmith' from the day my Dad died; it was a title or rank, I feel). I said I would. His next question was: 'How much are you going to charge me?' That was one of the first mistakes I made. I said: 'How much did me Dad charge you?' '8/-,' he said, and I knew that he always paid cash. 'Right,' he said, and he paid me the price I asked. The proper price for shoeing a pony at that time was about twelve or fourteen shillings.

I had committed myself to charge 8/- I could not tell him different. As I looked at him, I thought that he looked old and wouldn't last long. The sequel is that Bill Allman lived many years. He had his pony shod about six times a year and never brought more than 8/-.

The price of shoeing by this time had gone up to about fifteen bob, but I could not bring myself to tell him any different. I must have lost about £20 over the years. He eventually died like we all must and he requested that I be one of his bearers, so I had to take a couple of hours off as well to go to his funeral! But, Bill Allman was truly a great country character and if I did lose a bob or two shoeing his pony I am sure I learned a lot from him and characters like him. I can see him now, trotting off to Ellesmere with pony and trap; lugging hay in the field by us, or walking a cow home to where he lived by Frankton Station from a field on the Perthy, 'the Long Acre'. As I write this story I wonder what he would have thought about inflation now, where in some cases prices can nearly double overnight.

If I left Bill Allman's story here I would do him a great injustice, for there is a sequel, for it was he who started me up in farming. Getting a bit more land is always a struggle. About a month or two before he passed way, he came into my smithy and said: 'Blacksmith, do you want a bit more land to farm?' 'Yes,' was my reply, then he said: 'I'm getting a bit weary and you want to be the first to ask the Landlord for it.' Getting more land meant a lot at that time, as I was farming 22 acres only and with a full time blacksmith job, life was being lived at a fair old pace. I went on my bike to see the Colonel (my car was off the road at the time), who at that time was still living in Hardwick Lodge, prior to moving back into Hardwick Hall. He agreed I could have the tenancy of the three acres when Mr. Bill Allman gave it up. This would now allow me to put on a bit of farm help as the extra land would keep a couple more cows. Land was very hard to come by even in those days as every farmer was trying to expand their farms to produce more. So Bill Allman gave me the chance to be the first to ask for his three acres. I remember my mistake about the 'patches' referring to his four fields. One day he was at the smithy waiting for a pony to be shod. There were two or three horses waiting their turn ahead of him so I said: 'Go and put your pony in one of your little patches, and I will fetch him later in the day and shoe him for you, to save you waiting.' He looked at me and in front of two or three other farmers, said: 'I have four fields not patches.'

He took me down a peg or two, but it was a good country lesson taught by an older character, and one that I have remembered ever since. Who was it that said, never judge a man by the clothes he wears? (I think that could also include these days, 'Never judge a man by the size of farm he farms, or the car he runs, or the size of business he owns').

Soon after my Father died two travelling gypsies were passing through. They called at the smithy and wanted four shoes put on their horse. They did not ask the price, neither did I think to tell them. However, I shod the horse. The older and bigger of the two asked in a rough voice how much it was. 'Fourteen shillings,' I said, which was the proper price and a fair charge at that time. 'You'll be bloody lucky,' he said. 'I've never paid more than 10/-.'

I said: 'Well, it looks as though you will have to.'

'No bloody chance,' he said. 'You'll have 10/- or nothing.'

I looked at them. 'God,' I thought, 'they look like big devils to argue with,' but I realised that if I let them get away with it, the news would soon spread that I could be frightened. 14/- was a lot of money. I told them the horse would not go out of my shop until I had been paid the proper price. They both seemed to come closer. 'Here goes,' I thought, 'I am for a bloody good hiding as well.'

Then I realised I had my shoeing hammer in my hand. 'The first one to raise a hand to me will get this hammer full in the face,' I let them know. It seemed to check them in their stride because they realised I meant it. Uttering more oaths, the big bloke said he was not paying that price. Realising they were not as tough as they looked my courage was returning. I said: 'Tell you what, I will fight you, double or quits, £1. 8s. 0d or nothing.' Thank God, he didn't take me on! He still insisted he was not paying that price.

'O.K.,' I said, 'I am not bothered,' remembering Dave Evans. 'I will take the shoes off and your horse can go barefoot.'

I picked up my shoeing tools, picked the horse's foot up, but before I could start to take the shoes off, his mate said: 'Pay the bugger and let's go.' The bigger of the two then threw the 14/- onto the smithy floor and I was not too proud to pick it up. I can't remember if they said goodbye or no, but I don't mind admitting I felt pretty scared. None of their mates ever tried to get their horses done any cheaper with me. They had probably been sent to try me out.

One morning I got up and went outside to investigate a familiar sound. Standing in my smithy was a horse I recognised as belonging to Mr. Walley of Lower Frankton — a distance of about a mile and a half from the smithy. The horse had no shoes on, indeed had not been shod for some time due to the arrival of another tractor on Mr. Walley's farm.

During the day I put four shoes on the old horse, thinking one of the farm chaps had left it there for me to shoe, and would be collecting him later on. One thing puzzled me — the horse was not tied up. It had no halter or bridle on. It was still standing there at seven o'clock that night; tied up to the old oak tree adjoining our smithy. About 8 o'clock that night Mr. Walley arrived in his car. Coming into the smithy he said to me: 'I wondered where the old horse had got to. I've been looking for him all day: I've decided, as he is getting past work to sell him to be slaughtered.'

As he looked at the old lad, he said: 'Alf, you've put a set of shoes on him.'

I said: 'He was here first thing this morning, I thought one of your chaps had brought him to be shod, so I shod him.'

'Well Alf,' he said, 'You've saved his life. If he had enough sense to come here on his own, wait all day long for me to find him, he can stay on for a while longer on my farm.'

Be it known, that old horse stayed on Mr. Walley's farm for many years, in a long and happy retirement. In spite of all the years that I have been connected with horses, I believe a horse knows when he is going to be put down, as my Dad's old pony a few years before knew his time had come.

A few weeks after Dad died, a farmer arrived at the smithy with a plough on the back of his cart, I recognised it immediately, — it was a one-way horse drawn plough, a Davy Sleep, by make or name.

The farmer said: 'I have brought you this plough back, I was going to buy it off your Dad but don't want it now.'

'What do you mean,' I said. 'You agreed to buy it off me Dad for £2.

'Ah, but I don't want it now,' he said again.

I said: 'You have had it for twelve months, and now you say you don't want it? What can I do with it now? everybody is changing over to tractor ploughs.'

'Well, I dunna want it,' he said yet again, unloading it on the smithy bank.

Where's the one wheel and the suck off it?' I said. 'Oh, I took them off because they were off my own plough.' 'Well this plough is no good without them.' I said, 'It's only fit for scrap now.'

He left me fuming. The plough went into the scrap. No one else wanted it minus certain vital parts. Thank goodness all farmers were not like him (especially at that time in my business career). The life of the new village blacksmith would not have been as pleasant had they been.

In recording this last story and the story when my Dad and me were taken to court, I am only trying to illustrate that working for one's self is not always easy. But, one is, I feel, a better man for having a few knocks, it is part of going through the University of life.

New Year's Eve, after my Dad had died (no holiday on New Year's Day then), Charlie Butler and Wal Powell, who worked for Fred Griffiths the builder came into my smithy with a main drive casting off a concrete mixer, smashed into about five or six pieces.

'Can you get this welded and mended for 7.30 in the morning?' Charlie asked.

I looked at it and said: 'I canna perform a miracle.'

'Well if you canna mend it there will be about ten blokes standing still tomorrow. We canna get a new one, and the Boss dunna know we have broke it loading it on the wagon,' Wal Powell explained.

I started to repair the casting about 7 o'clock, and by the time I had finished and put it in the smithy fire to cool down slowly it was 12 o'clock. Up again at 6 o'clock next morning to make sure it was alright and ready for Charles and Wal to pick up at 7.30. They did so and no time was lost for the Griffiths' building firm.

The price I charged for that particular job, £1 5s. 0d, does not sound much by today's standards but I suppose it was the going rate in those days. I wondered how Fred Griffiths would take the bill, but it was paid.

Just before Mother went to live at Tetchill she still kept a few chickens in her old hen-pen down the garden. A rather brash chap came to work on a neighbouring farm, living in a cottage not far from us. He came to our door one night and said: 'I've lost one of my hens, can I go and have a look in your pen to see if she has gone in there?' I went with him and without any ceremony he grabbed the first hen on the perch. 'This is her,' he said, and away he went with the hen under his arm back to his cottage.

Two nights later, same procedure. Only my Mother was in at the time. She, I am sure was frightened of him, and let him take another hen. He must have watched for us lads going out because about two nights later he came again and took Mother's hen saying it was the same hen that kept coming back. My brother Frank and I decided, unbeknown to Mother, that the time had come to take drastic action, or else Mother would have no hens left.

That night after Frank had finished his tea, we both went to this fellow's cottage. I said to Frank: 'You stand back away from the door, don't let him see you but be ready if he decides to be awkward as he is noted for being a rough handful.' I knocked his door. He opened it; he was about 6ft 2ins. and weighed about 16 stone. He looked quite a giant in the flickering light of the oil lamp on his kitchen table.

'What do you want?' he said.

'I've come to tell you,' I said, 'if you take anymore of Mother's chickens you'll be in trouble.'

'Oh,' he said. 'Who from?'

'Me,' said I. At that he took a step forward and took a swing at me, which I fortunately ducked. As he lurched forward, Frank came from out of the shadow to help me, thank goodness. On seeing Frank he immediately dived back to get into the house, slipped and fell against the kitchen table almost causing the light to wobble over. His wife slammed the door in our faces and bolted it from the inside, — not that I had any intention of trying to get inside his house.

When I got home I realised that my hat had come off in the scuffle, so I said to Frank: 'We'll go and get my hat tomorrow night, let him cool down a bit first.' I wasn't going to lose my hat as well as two or three chickens. Next night Frank came home from work at Ellesmere Post Office.

'Right,' I said, 'Let's go and get my hat.'

'There is no need to,' said my Mother, 'Jack has fetched it, he has more sense than you pair put together.'

On reflection it was as well, but that fellow never came again for hens, or 'owt else.

My Landlord, the then Major Kynaston (now Colonel), bought a big brand new Hunter Super Snipe, a beautiful black car, I suppose one of the most expensive cars that had ever been to our smithy. He brought it up and left it one Saturday morning for a tow-bar. Jack and I made one and put it on.

For what reason, I don't know, but we decided to take a ride in this magnificent motor car as far as Halston Back Gates. I suppose the temptation was too much. We both felt like landed gentry waving to the villagers we met as we sped along the main road.

We gave no thought to what the consequences might have been had we damaged it, we both could have been turned out of our house and blacksmith shop. Luckily we arrived home safe and sound.

On a wet afternoon reliving my memories I realise no one can take them away. Often through the years when the Colonel went past in that beautiful car, I used to feel like telling everyone in my smithy I had driven it. I doubt if they would have believed me.

When I recall that story I realise the village blacksmith was one of the most adaptable persons in the community, for as well as being able to shoe a horse, he had to be able to put a drawbar on a motor car, worth at today's price £15,000. At the other end of the scale many car springs I have made out of old cart springs, when there was a shortage of new material (seven shillings and sixpence would be charged for making a main leaf and resetting a car spring, a small price for keeping a vehicle on the road. Now something like £12 to £14 per hour is the charge for labour alone).

Chapter 14

'First I Take To B.V.T.'

SHORTAGE of money was very evident throughout my youth and early twenties. Many were the gallons of petrol Dave Walley or Ron Hodnett, two of my mates, pinched from their dad's vehicles to allow us to go to dances in other villages. Syphoning petrol can be tricky. My car was a Ford-Eight, one of Henry Ford's £100 cars.

It had one of the old felt roofs which had rotted, as it had been standing for about five years before I bought it. With a lot of bargaining I got it for £12 10s. 0d., — quite a lot of money in those days; to me, it was a small fortune. How proud I was of owning my own car even if it had no seats or roof. Eric Jones the joiner came with me to fetch it (he and Ron his son have been great friends of mine, always).

We took an old beer crate to sit on to drive it home, all the way from Gobowen. We managed to switch the ignition on with a horse nail and Eric gave me a tow towards Frankton. All the way to Whittington I kept trying to start it in gear, and suddenly she (it must have been a 'she') burst into life near Halston Back Gates. Smoke was billowing out like a ship's funnel or a smoke screen. After the first minute or two the smoke became less and there in all its glory was my own first go-able motor car, but without a licence or insurance, and not much petrol either. We were all the same in

105

that respect in those days! I still remember the number forty years later — BVT 401.

It was not long before BVT 401 was christened by the rest of the village as the 'blacksmith's very touchy BVT).

As proud of BVT as I was, I did not realise the many hours of enjoyment I would spend around Shropshire roads and lanes with this wonderful machine. There was no need to worry about losing ignition keys, a No. 8 horse nail would switch her on and off. I managed to find some old seats and Eric fixed them in.

Still no roof! I went for some petrol, after he had put 1½ gallons in the tank the garage man said: 'Alf, you've got no top'. Thinking he was taking the mickey I said: 'Aye, it blowed off along Halston Bank.' But he was being friendly, — he meant a top on my petrol tank; we had a laugh about that. A flat piece of galvanised sheet was screwed on to the roof, a bit of gas tar slapped on, and we were ready for any storm. Aunty Sally, who had been a seamstress in her younger days, came to stay for a couple of days with Mother and she lined the interior with an old army blanket (all the way from Burma).

One outing I remember clearly was the night five of us went to a dance at Holt in my pride and joy. Dave Walley, Jack Haynes, Ron Hodnett, Edgar Jones and myself. I had been having a bit of trouble with the light fuses, to stop them blowing. I put in a bit of welding wire in three places, because it was stronger than fuse wire. I did not think to try the lights before setting off. We arrived at Holt in daylight; had our usual drink at the White Lion and on to the dance in the Kenyon Hall. We started for home around midnight, switching the lights on by Rothwell's Garage. Of course, the welding wire was too strong, all the bulbs went! We pulled in to the side — twenty miles from home.

Jack Haynes had a brainwave, he volunteered to sit on the bonnet, with his torch. Brilliant idea! Ex-R.A.F. electricians thinking! We got him perched on the bonnet and started off, when it decided to belt down with rain. After about two miles he was wet through and unable to see much so we decided to get him back in the car. Suddenly it stopped raining and the moon started to shine. There was no traffic about (petrol was still rationed).

I decided to head for the Perthy quietly, with Jack Haynes

complaining bitterly about his wet clothes. We got as far as Overton, seven miles from home. There had been something on in the Cocoa Rooms, crowds of people still about. I threaded my way quietly through the many shouts of: 'Where's your blooming lights?' and I managed to get on to the Ellesmere road which I knew well.

We were met by a police car who had passed us before, the driver realised we had no lights, — at that moment the moon seemed to shine a bit brighter and my foot went down a bit! With my £12/10- motor car I decided to make a run for home! The police car had to go to Overton to turn, giving me a good start.

As we were coming past the Trotting Mare pub Ron Hodnett in the back said: 'He is gaining on us.'

Realising the consequences if I were caught I made a big decision. About four hundred yards from the pub is a right turn for Criftins, this I took at God knows what speed, on two wheels, I reckon, at one stage. Luckily for us the police car went straight on towards Ellesmere. We came in the back way home through Criftins. We met one other car with great big headlights; we could not see a thing. The other driver put his head through his window and said: 'Did you know you've got no lights on that damn thing?' I said: 'Thank you for telling me, I didn't know!'

By now it was quite moonlight. We met a fellow with a fag, and Jack spluttered: 'That beggar's got more lights than us.'

We arrived home at the Perthy in one piece, I did not think I was doing wrong at that time, but on reflection it was really a stupid thing to do. *My Mother* would have taken my licence off me, had I been caught, never mind the police! I don't know who these young 'uns of today think they are, belting down the main road in their modern cars, but I bet they don't have any more fun than we did, even if we did have to start 'her' with a horse nail.

My brother Frank and I went to New Brighton, by Liverpool (not the Wrexham one), one night with 'her' to a 'Welcome Home' party for my cousin, Jack Davies, at the Riverside Restaurant. There was a terrific spread of food by our standards, and cigars on the tables as well. I remember pinching a couple of cigars, and putting them in my top pocket of my jacket. We stayed the night at my Aunty Sally's in Wallasey.

We started home next morning, got as far as Marford Hill, the other side of Gresford, when the 'old girl' stopped dead! Neither of us was very mechanically minded but we had the bonnet up looking for the trouble when up comes a bloke on a bike, an obvious mechanic. 'Broke down lads?' he said. 'I dunna know what's the matter with her, just stopped,' I said. 'There's petrol in her alright,. he continued. He checked the plugs, then the distributor, and found a wire broken in the distributor, mended the break, gave her a swing with the starting handle, and she roared into life. 'Thanks very much,' I said, 'How much do we owe you?' 'Nothing lads,' he said, 'Glad to be of help.' 'We're very grateful to you,' I said, 'Do you smoke?' 'Only Woodbines,' was the reply. 'Here,' I said, 'Have a couple of cigars,' remembering the cigars I had in my top pocket. I can still see the look of amazement on his face as we drove off, — two 'oud country lads with two cigars in their pockets!

Chapter 15

'But Saturdays Still Reserved for A Kick'

FRANKTON FOOTBALL CLUB was reformed in 1946. The lads were now all back from the forces. At a meeting in the billiards room of Frankton Parish Hall, a committee was formed. Mr. Percy Walley, a local farmer, was elected Chairman, Jim Brayne, Secretary, Dai Phillips, George Brayne, Hayden Gregory, Harold Coles, Tom Haynes and Dick Dutton were the other members of the committee.

Fund raising efforts were held to buy kit, shirts and footballs being the first priority. Supply your own knickers, boots, stockings, pads, etc., were the order of the Committee. Friendlies were held through that summer against Ellesmere, Whittington, Army teams from Park Hall and Otley, and Halston, which still had soldiers there. Both had been American bases through the war up until 'D' Day. Halston pitch was the field on the right up Hindford Lane, now farmed by Brian Lea.

We did quite well in the trial matches and friendlies, but then came the moment of truth. We joined the Oswestry and District League and the first two fixtures were against St. Martins Miners, away, and the return at home on Hardwick Park the following week. Why we played them twice in the league two Saturday's following, I don't know. We arrived the first Saturday at St. Martins to find half their team had gone to play in a band contest with Ifton Brass Band, the Colliery Band, so we had a fair chance of beating them.

The result was a win for St. Martins 2-1. The following Saturday, we fielded the same team at home, but their much strengthened side, with the return of some of their best players, ran rings around us. We lost 6-2, it could have been more.

The following played for Frankton Football Club at that time:

Den Coles, Brian Jones, Alf Strange, Jack Strange, John Hayward, Bill Strange, Jack Nicholas, Phil Arthan, Jack Haynes, Tom Nicholas, Tom Edwards, Ted Timmins and Harold Davies.

The following Saturday, we lost to Ellesmere in the Shropshire Junior Cup. Gordon Drury scored three goals (one with his hand! Thirty eight years later, he has just admitted it!!) The next Saturday, we were away to Llanrhaeadr Y.M. We had a bus at Top Frankton, but no driver; Charlie Butler eventually drove. Away we went, arriving an hour late. We would have been fined today. Another defeat, 3-0. Brother Jack was hurt and was taken to the Orthopaedic Hospital, Gobowen. That was the end of his football career; no subs allowed in those days. Drastic measures had to be taken after, four defeats in a row, and a key man in hospital. The officials engaged George Antonio Rowlands who played inside-right for Stoke City to give us a tactical talk. The outside-right for Stoke City in those days was the great Stanley Matthews (now Sir Stanley — still coaching). George came to the Parish Hall to talk to a bunch of village lads all dead keen but fast losing heart after four defeats on the run. Out came the blackboard and we all listened intently to his talk.

The 'W' formation was to be the plan of attack for the following Saturday against Pant on the field at the back of Cross Guns pub (now built on). We arrived at Pant with renewed hope and inspiration after George's talk. Pant were just as determined as we were and they had a great centre-forward in Sid Pugh, and a good goalie called Len Griffiths. Play was fast and furious and with a few minutes left, the score was four goals each. Frankton were then awarded a pentalty. Who was to take it? We had never discussed that in our talk. As I was Captain, I decided I had better take it myself. Placing the ball on the spot, I realised Frankton's first victory depended on this. All our fifteen supporters on the line were there with bated breath.

110

I took a deep breath, retreated two or three yards, trotted forward and hit the ball. I remember it well. It went straight and true, missing the goal by a good five yards, — nearer the corner flag than the goal post. You could hear the groans back in Frankton. I felt terrible. Would I ever be able to hold my head up again in Frankton? All George Antonio's work gone to waste.

But all was not lost. From the goal kick the ball came to me. I trapped it, ran forward a few yards, lobbed the ball across to Ted Timmins who was unmarked. He hit it first time into the roof of the net, no time to centre the ball. A victory for Frankton at last, 5-4! We sang all the way home in the bus. There was as much jubilation as if we had won the F.A. Cup.

The following Saturday, Ellesmere again on the Park in a league match. We must have had a change of fortune at Pant. A victory this time against our arch rivals, and what's more my old boss, Dave Evans, at 49, was playing for Ellesmere. We were able to go for a drink to Ellesmere again holding our heads high. (We really were good friends, it was just that there was always a bit more needle in a local Derby).

Among those in their team that day were: Don Boyling, Jack Chadds, Gordon Drury, Dave Evans (my old boss) trying to outdo Stanley Matthews), and Bert Williams. They enjoyed their football just as much as we did. One of our favourite referees was Dai Lodwick from Oswestry. He always seemed to referee a couple of home matches when the snowdrops were out in Hardwick Woods. He would come off the two o'clock train, pick snowdrops, putting them in his case in bunches. We nicknamed him the 'Snowdrop Referee'. He used to wear a schoolboy hat. Very fit he was and if you appealed for what you thought was an offside or a foul and he did not agree with you he would shout: 'Get on.' If my memory serves me right, he was still refereeing at the age of 65. What a sight he used to be tearing up Hardwick Park. I don't know, but there don't seem to be Dai Lodwick's around today.

The Frankton team operated until 1951. We had one or two hours of glory. The 1948 final of the Village Cup on Oswestry Town's ground against Weston Rhyn was one. With ten minutes to go, we were awarded a penalty, and Harold Davies to take it. He'd never missed a penalty in two seasons for Frankton. Up he stepped, hit the post and from the rebound Weston Rhyn came straight out to score the first of their two goals, Bob Turner scoring both of them.

The following year the same two teams were in the final again, this one being played at Chirk. With five minutes to go, John Hayward went through completely on his own, dribbled round the goalkeeper, who had come out, sent the ball goalwards, only to see Ralph Jones, the Weston Rhyn full-back making a save fit for any goalkeeper with his hands. He bounced the ball a couple of times like a proper goalie would do and punted up field. A blatant penalty! The referee ignored all our appeals for a penalty. He must have been blind and deaf. Ralph laughed his head off. A one-all draw. It was the end of the season, with no chance of a replay. We shared the Village Cup, six months each.

After two or three seasons in the Oswestry and District, the committee decided to join the Whitchurch and District League, probably because there would be less travelling expenses. However, our first game was against Bronington on the Park. The result was 4-1 in their favour, and doubts were expressed. That was to be our only defeat all season, one-all draw with Newton-on-the-Hill was our only other dropped point. So we became the first team to win the new cup that went with winning the League.

Towards the end of the season, we were getting short of players. I think we only had about thirteen to start with. Two or three injuries and we were struggling. Tom Speke's help was enlisted and he managed to get us three soldiers from Otley Camp. I remember them well, — Doug Slade, Johnny Aston's brother from Manchester United and another lad called Jock. These three lads were invaluable towards the end of the season. I remember we were relying on them for an evening match when we heard that Jock was confined to barracks for seven days. Tom Speke, who worked at Otley Camp was not to be deterred by such things as Army discipline. He told me: 'Have a car ready by Otley back gates, I will arrange something.' This I did and sure enough, Jock appeared as if by magic into my car, played his game and I had him back at camp straight after the game, no questions asked. Twenty Players' cigarettes was the price paid for Jock's services that evening. Sham amateurism rearing its ugly head on the playing fields of rural Shropshire, at that early date!

We played an exhibition match at Whitchurch when we went to

collect our Cup. Champions against the pick of the League. At least 500 people came to see it. I'm not sure of the result but we received the Cup at the end of the game as Whitchurch League Champions for the 1949/50 season.

Coming back to Ellesmere to celebrate at the Market Hotel Frankton's adopted pub, we had a great time, only marred by a certain Sergeant Major Hooper. In the pub he had noticed that one of his lads, Jock, had his top button of his tunic undone. As we trooped out to get fish and chips from Sal Chadwick's up St. John's Hill (there were only two fish and chip shops in Ellesmere at that time, Ike Price's in Watergate Street and Sal's up the hill, Sal's was the nearer), he stopped our footballer, his soldier.

He told Jock he was being put on charge for being improperly dressed and he was to appear before the Camp Adjutant at 9 o'clock on Monday morning, which I suppose would mean seven days confined to barracks for him. Poor Jock! What an end to a very happy day and season.

We got our fish and chips and a few of us decided that we would have to intervene in this unjust charge.

The following night, a Sunday, after Chapel, two or three of us went down to Ellesmere, knowing the Sergeant Major would be in the Market Hotel — his usual haunt. A good 6ft. he was and as bad as all sergeant majors. I was to be spokesman. Hooper was there in his usual place. Taking a deep breath I said: 'Who do you think you are putting Jock on charge? Montgomery?' His reply was: 'Mind your own bloody business and don't interfere with Army Regulations.' 'It is my business,' said I, 'Jock played football for Frankton, and if he hadn't, he would not have been improperly dressed. Will you drop the charge?'

'Bugger off back, you bloody country yokels. Get off back and comb the straw out of your hair!'

'O.K., we'll do that but before we go, just listen to what I have to say. If you dunna drop that charge on Jock, you could well find yourself chucked into the Mere one night. We inna frightened of NO bombastic Sergeant Major. We might be from the country, but I'm warning you, this could easily befall you one night.'

Mind you, I know that there were about four of us together at that time. He went rather quiet and we decided to let the matter drop

113

and await the results of our endeavours. We went down to Ellesmere again on the Tuesday to find out what, if anything, had happened to Jock. The first lad we bumped into in the town was Jock. We asked what had happened but he said he didn't know. He had heard no more about the charge, only that the reason he was NOT being charged was due to 'civilian influence'. We saw the Sergeant Major many times after. He never seemed to look quite so big or tall again. I often wonder if we would have carried out our threat to chuck him in the Mere. Forty years have passed since that incident. If I were ever to see any of those lads again or the Sergeant Major, a drink together would be the best thing.

The Village Cup team always had to consist of lads who lived within a mile radius of club headquarters. Our H.Q., Frankton's Parish Hall at the top of the Brow, meant that we could not include Phil Arthan who lived at Pentre Morgan near St. Martin's. However, a major decision was taken by the committee to move Headquarters to Mrs. Dutton's of Old Marton! This enabled us to get both Phil and Jeff Mollineux within the mile radius. A 'tactical move' so to speak. The Frankton Village Cup side was:

> John Price; Dennis and Brian Jones, Brow Farm; John Hayward, Bottle Row; Ted Timmins, Chapel House; Harold Davies, 6 Higher Perthy; Phil Arthan, Pentre Morgan; Jeff Mollineux (nicknamed Bugsy), Canal Cottage; Frank and Alf Strange, Perthy Smithy, and John Clay, Crickett Farm.

I think the Village Cup radius rules often used to be broken. I remember once we were to play Ruyton-XI-Town and included a couple of Army lads from Otley — we didn't even know their names. Another time, I remember Duncan Jones, who lived in Ellesmere, playing for Criftins. He had married a Criftin girl and was supposedly sleeping at his mother-in-law's at Criftins, but was seen going late one night into his own house in Ellesmere.

'Protests', ' illegal players', 'subs', 'sweepers', 'strikers', 'centre-backs', '5-3-2 formation', were new terms to us, or terms we disregarded, it was the 'kick' we wanted. Showers, baths? — Not on your nelly, never 'eard of them, buckets of cold water and think yourself lucky to have a game; and in 1947, cold was as cold as it ever was!

To be able to play on Hardwick Park at Frankton was reward enough.

I did have about ten games for Oswestry Town, then in the Birmingham League, at right full-back. George Davies played right-half. I came back to play for Frankton, he went to play for Sheffield Wednesday, but our paths had crossed.

We would work until one o'clock on Saturdays in those days. Kick-off would be at two in winter (no floodlights, even in English League soccer). Many times I have run down our field at ten to two with a butty in my hand for a two o'clock kick-off. And then the bombshell. Rumour had been rife for some time that the Colonel was going to plough up the Park. George Brayne had been told and so had Dai Phillips, who worked on the Estate. We kept hoping that it was only a rumour, but in vain. That was the end of Frankton football team. No other field could be found, despite desperate attempts. Farming was becoming intensive. Nobody wanted twenty-two players kicking the grass off, never mind the followers, cheering it in anguish.

Sitting here writing on a cold winter's night, I can relive those times over and over again. I can picture Frankie Morris tearing down the left wing; recall Phil Arthan arms and legs flailing like windmills — there was NO way you could knock him — to try and get round him took minutes.

I can see again the sliding tackles made by John Clay — today's referees would run out of yellow cards! We had never heard of any law which said 'No touching the goalie' — they were likely, given half a chance, to land in the back of the net, ball and all!

Rubber studs? Plastic Pitches? The thought makes me laugh. The wetter the ground the better you could slide 'um! Leather balls, heavy as anvils would very near knock your neck in if you happened not to head it right.

Half-time tea, made by Mrs. Brayne of Hardwick, was under the larch tree; kit washed by Mrs. Jim Brayne. Theo Jones ran his car to fetch the refs., at times, as well as players. What a back-up team we had. None better in the First Division today. Tom Haynes, who himself had been a good footballer, ran the line, Mrs. Butler, Mrs. Jim Brayne were the cheer leaders, shouting at visiting supporters, as well as telling the referee what they thought of him. What a long way off that seems now. Wrecking trains, hooliganism, stabbing one another? Our football was played hard but fair. No favours given or expected. But we always had Hardwick Pool, when at home, to cool the ref. down if he got too hot.

Where are we going? Where have we gone wrong? I know that too much is expected nowadays for too little, for one thing. One match a week with all the training facilities at their disposal. I once remember playing three games one Easter Monday. Morning, afternoon and early evening as well as doing a week's work. I am sure that we got a lot more enjoyment out of our football then, than the youth of today get out of theirs.

Many of those who made it all possible for a few short years just after the war have passed on, but a few of us still left with our memories. Were we really as good as we thought we were? How would we fare against the average village side of today (if there is such, with no imported players). One can never know, 'cos I'm too 'owd to put my boots on, once more.

A few years ago we did all get together, the original Frankton team, well, about eight of us, with the rest being made up of youngsters to help out, and played a trial match against a potential Frankton XI who were trying to form a team. The result was 4-0 to us, half an hour each way. It seemed like four hours. Would the ref. never blow his whistle? What we lacked in pace, we made up for in skill — passing instead of running.

Many times they challenged us again when they had more experience, but we were content to rest on our laurels!

I know we all suffered weeks of agony from aching muscles that we never knew we had. I also played odd games for other teams in different leagues to us. Wem Town, Wem White Stars, Welshampton, Ellesmere, Overton. One game sticks in my memory, well, two actually, — well two becomes four, just like that.

One was the night I was asked to play for Ellesmere against Oswestry Town on the Victoria Road ground at Oswestry. A strong side was Oswestry, with Ellesmere very much the underdogs. We were leading 1-0 with a few minutes to go, then Gordon Rogers equalised for Oswestry. A hotly disputed goal but, nevertheless, it was left to stand. A 1-1 draw. I am sure that Ellesmere would have settled for that having been beaten at home early in the season by Oswestry 8-1. The Ellesmere team realised that we were on a hiding to nothing, rose well to the occasion and played well as a team. The Ellesmere team was:

Ivor Powell; Bert Williams; Don Boyling; Gordon Jeffrey; Alf Strange; Jack Tudor; Gordon Drury; Derek Bell; Bill Mottram; Ken Lindop and Frankie Morris. Trainer: Charlie Harry. Chairman: Bill 'fix it' Jones.

I believe there were in excess of 1,000 spectators for that end of season game.

Another easily remembered, is one I played for Oswestry Town Reserves, against Shrewsbury Town Reserves. The Victoria Road ground at Oswestry was being levelled and it was being played on the field at the cemetery end. My brother Frank was playing for Oswestry at that time. I went to watch him play, and had stopped in Barley Mow, down Salop Road, for a pint of beer, arriving at the ground just in time for kick-off. Jack Howells told me they were a man short and asked if I would play. 'No chance,' I told him, 'I've had a drink of beer, and you can't play on beer.' He assured me I would be alright and that I would soon 'run it off'. Like a fool, I let him talk me to play right-half and I had not been on the field two minutes when I achieved immediate success. The ball came out from their defence, I got it in our own half, ran about 15 yards forward avoiding a couple of tackles, looked up and let fly from about 40 yards. I think I intended to pass it to the far post but it went like a rocket into the top corner of the net. What a start! That was all I did for the rest of the match. The beer took its toll on my wind and if it had been played today I would certainly have been substituted. I enjoyed my little bit of limelight although it was very short-lived.

September 15th, 1951, I was married and part of my marriage vows was to give up football for good. A small blacksmith business and a little farm to run were quite demanding on my time and Vera didn't want a lame husband to look after.

But once again, common sense did not prevail. I went with Frank to watch him play for Dudleston Heath, this time at Overton. The same old procedure, — one short — I made up the eleven and was picked to play the following week as well. Like a fool, I couldn't say 'No'. Harry Barkley pressured me. It was against Treflach, away, in some cup or other. With two minutes to go, Treflach and

117

Dudleston were all square, one each. A penalty was awarded to Tre-flach, but Ivor Powell, the Dudleston Heath goalkeeper saved the spot kick. The replay was to be at Dudleston Heath the following Saturday, and I was again persuaded to play despite my protests. Half an hour of play left, there was a long ball out of their defence. With not a soul near me, I went to head it back towards their goal. I mis-timed it, landed awkwardly and knew immediately something serious had happened. I tried to carry on for a second or two.

Ron Scott said I was wasting time, saying there was nothing the matter. Phil Morgan brought me home in his car. I had fifteen cows to milk by hand. Vera had never milked a cow . . . now was her time to learn! ! She did, and with the help of my brother and neighbours, we managed to carry on for sixteen weeks with me in plaster.

How I suffered about those marriage vows. That was the last game of football that I was to play. I thought the world had come to an end. The Insurance money was £2 a week, making £32 for the six-teen weeks, from the Dudleston Heath Insurance, my own personal accident Insurance brought in about another £2 a week from the Farmer's Union, — £80 for sixteen weeks. Ah well, lesson learned the hard way.

I blame Ivor Powell. If he hadn't saved that penalty we would not have had to replay and it would never have happened! However, I wouldn't have missed my football for all the tea in China. It's nice to look back now and recall mainly happy memories of meetings in our village smithy, arguements in Theo. Jones's the cobbler's shed, blaming one another when we lost, but remaining friends through all the adventures.

Frankton selectors were Di. Phillips, Jim Bryan, George Brayne and Dick Dutton. Towards the end of a season many is the time they would come to me and say: 'We've had a selectors' meeting and we have only got nine players, you'll have to find another two.'

Frankton's biggest defeat was against Oswestry Rovers, a pub team run by Tom Ince who used to keep the Star pub up Bailey Street. I think he had been a professional himself, but played for Oswestry on what you called a 'K form' in those days. His team beat Frank-ton 8-1 — a photograph of the team is included in this book. Ron Leonard scored about four; but in fairness to Frankton, we did end up with nine men.

Frankton's biggest win was against Salopian Engineers 14-1 and I scored an own goal for them by sending John Price the wrong way with a back pass.

Six medals and little cups are all I have to show for my football endeavours — and a left knee that goes in and out every so often! And a host of happy memories that I have had for the last forty years or so of the many players I played with.

One more story I remember — Frankton were a man short. The only available man on the line was Len Gregory, then in his forties. The committee were trying to get him to play. He was a very heavy smoker, somewhere in the region of 80 a day. How could he possibly play for an hour and a half without a fag?

Then somebody suggested that if he played on the left-wing two or three of them would be at regular intervals along the line with a fag so that he could have a draw in between attacks on the opponent's goal. Len did play, how many drags he had I don't know. Who knows, if he had not been such a heavy smoker, Liverpool may have snapped him up! His brother, Haydn, who was older than Len, once played when he was also well in his forties. I also recall Fred Stockton playing once at 50, when we were short, against Porthywaen on the Park.

Chapter 16

'Cricket In Overalls'

FRANKTON CRICKET TEAM was formed in 1950 though before that we had formed a knock-out team, eight-a-side to play in the Ellesmere Knock-Out on the Wharf Meadow. We called ourselves the Perthy Spivs. (Spiv was a name that was quite commonly used in those days, due to a black market term for shady dealers in foodstuffs, etc.) We were a very naive outfit as regards the finer arts of cricket etiquette. All we knew was that the ball was to be hit as hard and as often as possible. Straight bat play was a different game to that played by us Perthy lads. Just how naive we were regarding the finer points of the game has to be explained. Having your own bat and pads; owning a white pullover, never mind a sleeveless one were a mystery to us. Our overalls had to suffice for us.

In one knock-out match, Ted Timmins bowled in football boots. Talk about Trueman's foot drag! Or Willis's follow-through. Bill Lloyd the umpire, was left speechless, and that was something: he's the one who used to answer the remark, — 'I wasn't bloody well out.' with 'You look in Wednesday's *Advertizer* to see whether you was or not.' But many of the other teams in the first Ellesmere knock-out after the war were no better. A couple of bats and a ball was all the kit used in most games.

The first Ellesmere Knock-Out after the war was held on Wharf Meadow at the rear of United Dairies. Teams from local pubs and surrounding villages were invited to enter a team of eight players; the eighth man would bat on his own as long as there were overs to spare. I think about sixteen teams entered.

We, as I have said, went under the name of Perthy Spivs. Other teams had names like, 'Have-a-Goes'; 'White Lion'; 'Creamy Bits' (a team from the dairies, whose land we played on, now built on); Bolivers Colts (named after Jack Boliver who used to sell draw tickets. I can hear him shouting now 'Twenty Players, who wants them?'); 'The Fox Pub — Criftins'; 'Ron's Dons'; 'The Banks'; 'The Newnes' Wanderers'; 'Horse Menders'; 'The Methodists'; 'The Farmers'. Fine sounding names for teams keen on winning but intent on playing the game fairly and enjoying a pint and good company afterwards.

In the first round we were drawn against 'The Banks' a team consisting of bank employees and officials, immaculately dressed with blazers and cravats. They even had their own cricket bag etc. What a rag-a-muffin outfit we were by comparison. The pundits gave us no chance, a proper 'book' was being run and we were definitely the rank outsiders. But never underestimate a lad from Frankton who has played his cricket on Joe Strange's field at the back of the Smithy, complete with that 'stuff'. Our plans, indeed our only plan, was to attack and play cricket the only way we knew. When batting, hit the ball and run for everything, when fielding, stop everything possible, or run like the devil after 'it'.

We batted first. O. A. Davies, their opening bowler, was tall, quick and looked as if he had played for the M.C.C. He was nick-named 'Killer' Davies. Would we last two overs against him if he got a length? 'Dunna let him get on a length,' said Tom Speke. 'Down the wicket to him,' said Jack Haynes. 'Nay, dunna go back on your stumps,' said Wal Powell. So much advice was handed round. I think that we were all trying to give one another a bit of dutch courage. However, our plans or somebody's plan worked. 'Killer' Davies set his field, wicket-keeper about eight yards back, slips the same, hardly any fielder in front of the wicket. Tom Speke was to open for us and took his guard about a yard out. First ball was over pitched. He straight-drove it for a four. Who was the most surprised, him or the bowler I don't know, but that seemed to set the seal. If Speke could hit him for four we all could, and did, if my memory

121

serves me right. We scored about 80 runs all out in about 16 overs. Would that be enough of a target for the Bank's batsmen. As it turned out it was. We won quite comfortably. Our fielding and bowling was on top form.

We reached the final in the first year. The other team in the final was the 'Have-a-Goes'. The Captain, Gordon Drury, who pushed that goal in with his hand, had Doug. Owen, Jack Powell (Blackin), Jack Sproston, Dick Hampson (Gurney), Gordon Sproston, Bob Griffiths and Jack Ralphs in his team.

The Perthy Spivs were: the four Stranges, Jack, Bill, Alf and Frank, Tom Speke, Wal. Powell, Jack Haynes and Ted Timmins. There was a great crowd on the rails of Wharf Meadow on the first night of the final. We batted first and it was a shambles. None of us could get going at all. We were all out for a miserable 25 runs. Our supporters were stunned. The bubble had burst.

In went the 'Have-a-Goes' for their innings, cock-o-hoop. Everything seemed to go right for them, and we were knocked all over the meadow. 85 runs they made giving them a lead of 60-odd runs in the first innings.

The next night, the 'Have-a-Goes' were to bat first. If they did the same thing again, they would have a lead of 140-160, an impossible task for the Spivs.

We were not dismayed. We had a few breaks and got a couple of early wickets and had them all out for 19 runs, the lowest total of the whole knock-out.

This left us to get about 80 to win. Not an impossible task but sadly we were still about 15 short at the end of our allocated overs.

Nevertheless, Frankton's honour had been restored. We had given a good account of ourselves in the first Ellesmere Knock-Out after the war beating some good teams on the way to the final, but had not been quite good enough to win.

After going for a drink with the winners, we arrived home at the Perthy disappointed but not disgraced. My Mother, who had been waiting for us, said the team could finish off the barrel of home brew as we had finished our hay harvest, but I think there was more in it than she thought and there were some bad 'heads' in the morning.

Wal. Powell I believe got into his bed the wrong road round and blamed Marie his wife for moving the bed round. Happy, humble days they were!

Sadly Wharf Meadow has been nearly all built on, but the memories of older Ellesmere people and those of the surrounding villages linger on of football matches, Whit Monday Sports, the fairs at night, and the cricket knock-out, on it.

The Whit Monday Sports was a national event. Runners and bike riders would come from all over the country and from as far away as Manchester to pit their skills at Ellesmere. Chris Chataway of four-minute-mile fame, ran in the mile at Ellesmere Sports when he was stationed at Park Hall Camp doing his National Service. The little town of Ellesmere had its fair share of glory on a par with some of the bigger towns of our country.

We had the Brown Bomber himself, Joe Louis, here, landing on a field used as an airstrip near Halston Hall Camp when the Americans were based there.

Ellesmere Cricket Knock-Out continued for years, and I think Perthy Spivs reached the final a couple more times, without ever winning it, always the bridesmaid, never the bride!

Jack Haynes had a brain wave as the venue had now been changed back to Ellesmere Cricket Ground up Birch Road. Why not change our name from Perthy Spivs to Hardwick Fiddlers after our ground at Hardwick Park. This we did with great success and if my memory serves me right we won the Ellesmere Knock-Out three times but with a greatly different team: This time it was:

Ern. Davies, Bunty Bailey (both from Overton), Trevor Thatcher from Gobowen, Peter Done from the Black Lion Hotel in Ellesmere. Only four of the original team were left: Tom Speke, Jack Haynes, Jack Strange and me.

Not much of Perthy or Hardwick about that team. Then, teams were allowed to have just two 'star' players and that seemed to end the run of the Ellesmere Knock-Out. It never seemed the same. Teams were importing players from far afield and the local atmosphere went out of it. Perhaps we were as much to blame as the other teams by importing players to try and win. Oh, I almost forgot, towards the end of these knock-out games, the A.I. had a team, they were 'The Bull Boys'.

123

Arch. Morris from the Fox at Criftins ran a knock-out on a field at the back of his pub. That, I remember, brought some happy evenings for the villagers, and how handy to get a drink. The Fox Knock-Out ran for many years and I am sure there were many tales to tell of some of their matches. What a pity the local flavour seems to have gone out of those sort of evenings. As I remember, The Fox Knock-Out used to attract a few hundred spectators.

Chapter 17

'Still Three In The Nest'

THERE were three of us at home now living with my Mother, Jack, Frank and me. Frank had ended his National Service and was working in the office at the Co-op of Ellesmere. Jack was back at his blacksmith job at the new nationalised British Waterways in Ellesmere, and I was working the village Smithy as the blacksmith, as well as helping to milk our few cows, for my Mother.

The first upstairs when you were going out, was always the best dressed. We used to share the car on a rota basis, but Jack had bought a little Frances Barnet motor-bike, so this meant that Frank and I usually managed to have the car between us. Mother had never allowed any of us to have a motor-bike, she used to say: 'No lad of mine will have a motor-bike.' Somehow or other Jack managed to persuade her to change her mind, but he was about twenty-six years of age before she relented. He bought it from Harold Crossman's Garage in Oswestry. As Harold was selling it for somebody else, there was no guarantee; it was 'bought as seen' for £30.

We went for it on a Saturday afternoon; brother Bill was living in Oswestry at the time, in rooms with his wife Winnie. I picked him up after dropping Jack off at the garage, and took him to the garage. By this time, Jack had completed his dealings, and was trying to start the machine. 'Her' woudna start, so we gave him a push to get him going, and away he went.

We followed in the car, catching him up under the Works Bridge, stalled again, needing another push; After another couple of stops by Park Hall Camp, and another couple of pushes, she seemed to be going better.

Coming through Whittington by the Penrhos Pub, when Jack would be doing, I should think, about twelve miles an hour, a bloke came out of the yard on a push-bike; he passed Jack before he had reached the White Lion, another pub, about 200 yards away (before they altered the road at what was called the Three Trees turning).

Eventually we arrived home, it must have taken a good hour for six miles. 'Come and have a look at Jack's bike,' I said to Mother; she just gave me that steely look only Mothers can give: 'I dunna wanna see the blooming thing. I dunna know what his Dad would have said. I wish I adna give him permission to have it now.'

Just at that moment Jack would have agreed with her. However, we cleaned the bike up, put another plug in; changed the petrol which had a drop of oil added to it, and she seemed to sound a bit better.

'We will go and try her again,' said Jack. 'I'll come with you for a ride,' I said jumping on the back mudguard which had no seat, just a square grid frame to take a parcel. Away we went like hell down the Brow Bank as far as Hardwick Back Gates, turning there Jack shouted above the roar: 'I will try her right up the Brow Bank,' — quite a long steep hill about half a mile long.

Half way up she started to slow down, Jack changed down; about 200 yards from the top she started to slow down again. 'Change down,' I shouted. He shouted back: 'That's the last.' I jumped off, and she shot forward like a bullet without my extra weight. He had the engine done up and it went well for many years, but I don't think that bike would ever have won many races.

I was talking about this bike the other day to a bloke from Wem by the name of Mr. Wellstead who lived in Ellesmere before the war; he took over the story about motor-bikes by relating his own tale:

'I once passed your Dad in a pony and trap at the bottom of the Brow Bank on me motor-bike gong too fast, I had to turn up the Perthy, and came off on some loose chippings on the corner, ripping the knees out of me trousers and grazed me arms as well, feeling quite sorry for myself.'

He went on: 'Just then your Dad came up in the pony and trap "Did you get it?"

'Get what?, I said, still feeling sorry for myself.

"What you was bloody asking for when you went past me too fast," 'your Dad replied'.

'If I was expecting any sympathy I certainly got none off your Dad that day.'

Going back to the first upstairs being the best dressed reminded me of the night it was my turn to have the car; Frank, had gone to another village close by and he and his girlfriend had decided to walk into Ellesmere. I had gone down to Ellesmere in the car. I met Frank hobbling along Cross Street.

'I said: 'What's the matter?'

'Do us a favour, lend me the car for tonight,' he answered.

I said: 'No it's my car and my turn to have it.'

He came back: 'You can have it all next week if you will just lend "her" me for tonight.'

'What's the matter?' I said.

'Well,' he said, 'I have Jack's best shoes on and they have rubbed me heels and I wunna be able to walk back home,' came his painful explanation.

'Alright,' I said, 'But perhaps that will teach you a lesson.'

Jack took size eight's Frank took size nine's!

Another time I was on my way to a dance in the Town Hall at Ellesmere, I looked everywhere for my navy-blue pullover to go with my blue suit. Frank had changed first and gone out. The only pullover I could find was very bright yellow, really bright, like a canary. I thought it would have to do and put it on under my jacket. I did not know that this pullover had been knitted for Frank by his girlfriend for his birthday. When I arrived at the dance wearing it, Frank was already there with the girl who had knitted it. He came straight across to me in quite a tear and said: 'What the hell are you doing with my best pullover on?' I said: 'Open your jacket!' And there was my best navy-blue pullover. 'Come on,' I said, 'Let's get to the cloakroom ! ! !'

The thing about brothers is *you* can say what you like about them, but heaven help anybody else who runs them down, — a bit like the Beverley Sisters.

Work was now fast changing, in the late forties, and the village blacksmith was having to change to cope; first electricity had arrived in our village and this meant buying an electric welder, a drill (just like the dentist at Oswestry!) and a grinder.

It also meant that I had to have help in the little village smithy. Dick Grindly, from St. Martin's joined the 'firm' by coming to work for me, a fully qualified farrier and blacksmith — 2/6d an hour, eight hours a day, 'till 12 o'clock on a Saturday, — £5 10/- a week was the going rate.

It meant two of us keeping 'on our toes', but fortunately he was also a professional boxer, in about the 10 stone range. He fought many times at Wolverhampton and Liverpool Stadium and had a bash at the Welsh Lightweight Championship. He came to work one morning with both his eyes bunged up and a nasty cut over one of them.

I said: 'How did you get on last night?' 'Oh, won quite easy,' he replied. 'I dunna know what the other bloke must look like,' I retorted, thinking about my pound of flesh, NOT his. Twice a week he went training to the hut at Queenshead near West Felton. I sometimes went with him; and Ron Hodnett. There were quite a few good boxers there in those days; Art Lewis was about the best local and most well known.

The most famous of them all was Dennis Powell, quite a good boxer who was, at one time, light-heavyweight Champion of Wales. He fought and beat George James, Welsh Champion, in the open-air at Oswestry football ground. A vast crowd saw the local lad from Llanymynech winning the fight; I remember it well, it really was an emotional moment for the locals in the early 1950s.

About then I remember having a practice round with Dennis Powell because he knew Dick, I was about $11\frac{1}{2}$ stone at the time, and I thought I was fit. It was to be one three-minute round. I lost count of the times he hit me; I know how many times I hit him, — *not once*. I was glad it was only a friendly spar. I can hear the wise cracks, — 'Send for T.C.' — T. C. Price was the cattle slaughterer, so well known at that time, that the initials identified the place.

Every night on his way home from school a little lad, Fred Powell, used to call at the smithy. Harry Benson, a local farmer, was there one night; He said to Fred: 'Fred, as your name is Powell, are you any relation to Dennis Powell the boxer?' The little fellow thought for a minute and replied: '*No, but me Dad is!*'

Dick used to stand Fred on the anvil and get him to shout 'Rocco', the name of the local ice-cream man. Fred would shout his head off, and Dick would say: 'Can you 'ear him, Alf?' 'Not very loud,' I would reply. 'You inna going to get a penny tonight if you canna shout louder than that, Fred me lad,' said Dick. (A penny would buy an ice-cream). Then Fred would summon all his strength, it's a wonder they could'nt hear him in Ellesmere. Dick Grindly is included here in 'the nest' because my Mother used to feed him as if he was one of us.

We three Strange lads used to play a regular trick on village lads, we would tell them that we would teach them to catch a rabbit. We told them to get a large stone, put some pepper on it, and the rabbit would come up, sniff the pepper, sneeze, and hit his head on the stone, knocking himself out. One of us would then, when they had done that, go and shoot a rabbit and place it by the stone ready for them when they came home from school. The look on their faces when they found the rabbit is indescribable.

Talking about rabbits reminds me of a rabbit catcher, Frank Skitt (He, I remember, came with me to see Dennis Powell box at Oswestry). One night, soon after in Ellesmere, Frank who was quite a character, said to me: 'Alf, I've bought a new bike, but it's too big for me, so I've loosed the tyres down so that I can reach the seat!'

He once had a bet with Phil Welch, as to who could drink most beer in two hours, the contest was arranged at the White Hart in Ellesmere, from 8 o'clock to 10 o'clock. Frank arrived at a quarter to eight, bought a pint; somebody said to him: 'I thought the contest did not start until 8 o'clock, Frank.' His reply was, 'I am just having this one, just to wet me whistle. Who won the contest? I don't know, I don't think anyone knew.

Another character around at that time, and for many years after, was Bill Goode. His dog was troublesome and not kept under proper control and after many warnings from neighbouring farmers, one took him to Court over an incident of the dog attacking his chickens. The Court was held at Overton; that morning, Bill rang the farmer to ask whether he was going to the Court. The farmer replied: 'Of course I am.' 'Well in that case,' Bill said, 'Could you give me a lift in your car then we can both go together!'

I was in his company one night in the Railway Hotel in Ellesmere; most times he was amusing company. This night he had been in rare form. It came time to go. He was taking a few bottles of beer home in an old corn sack he had tied somehow or other around his shoulders.

To get out of the bar in those days there were three steep steps, and Bill, with his hand on the door latch, turned to us to tell us: 'Lads', he said. 'The *Rev. Brighton once said to me,*' "William, be *careful where ye tread, lest ye fall.*" Letting go the latch he fell down the steps, landing with a heavy crash. We rushed to see if he was alright. 'Dunna worry about me lads, is the beer alright in me sack?' Assured that the beer was O.K. he picked himself up, got on his bike and rode away into the gloom for home.

Chapter 18

'Cricket In White Flannels'

FRANKTON CRICKET TEAM proper had Saturday fixtures, and very occasional Sunday ones — it was still frowned upon in our village to play Sunday cricket. Transport was the biggest problem soon after the war. Not many had cars then. Often we went to other clubs in an old London taxi driven by Fred Allen from Ellesmere, the 'paraffin man'. Sleigh's hearse was also hired out. It was a funny sensation riding in the back of a hearse. It had no windows and I remember going to play at the Orthopaedic Hospital and as we came off the ground people stood still and took their caps off in respect, not knowing that there was a bunch of Frankton Cricket Club lads in the back. Jack 'Barney' Jones's wagon was another form of transport. He had been luggin coal all week and then we had to ride in the back on a Saturday afternoon. Needless to say it had not been cleaned out and I once remember going to play at Hanmer. As they had not got a pavilion at Gredington Park where they played, we had to change into what whites we had before we left Frankton. What a state we were in when we got to Hanmer. Someone from Hanmer remarked that they thought they were playing Frankton and not the Black and White Minstrels.

I recall a funny incident at Hanmer. Ted Gough, a very good opening bat, used to play for Jimmy McAlpine's XI before the war, and you had to be good to get in that team. He was playing for

Hanmer and Peter Done was opening bowler for Frankton with Tom Speke as umpire.

Peter bowled, Ted played and missed. The ball hits him on the pad and some kid sitting on the boundary shouts 'How'z 'at?' Tom, lighting his pipe at the time, sticks his finger up and says 'Out.'

Ted protested, Peter Done asked Tom to change his decision but Tom was adamant. 'How was I out,' asks Ted. 'Because I said so,' declared Tom. Away went Ted as only a sportsman would.

Afterwards, Peter Done said to Tom: 'Tom, the ball was missing the wicket by a mile.' 'I know,' said Tom. 'But if I hadna give 'im out then he would have scored a lot of runs, — I had to take the first opportunity to get rid of him.'

Another incident involving Tom Speke was when he and Jack Haynes were batting together. Jack Haynes had scored quite a few and was batting quite well when he straight drove the ball. Tom Speke, at the other end, caught it, gave it to Den Drury, the bowler, who appealed for a catch as the ball had not been grounded. 'Out,' said Bill Lloyd the other umpire. Jack Haynes went, playing hell with Tom and calling him all sorts of names. Tom said: 'You'd bin in long enough Jack, give somebody else a bat.' (Cricket as it should be played).

In another game, playing Oswestry Tech at the Derwen ground, we had them all out for 20. Brother Bill, our Captain, said to George Brunt, their Captain: 'Shall we knock them off before tea and then have another match, so many overs apiece?' 'Okay,' said George, 'Suits us.' Frankton went in to bat to knock off the runs. All out for 17! Lost by three runs! What a funny game cricket can be!

Of all our fixtures my favourite was against Alberbury, which was a true village side and played cricket to enjoy it as we did, with a drink after in the Hand and Diamond. Many times I have come home to do the milking after staying for a drink with the Alberbury lads, — at ten o'clock at night!

Another fixture I used to enjoy was against Oswestry Second XI. Once I remember Edgar Cornes had got to 98. He had never scored a ton, and had played our bowling all over the ground. We didn't know where to put the fielders. My brother Jack decided to bring me on to bowl again. I had been fielding on the boundary, out of sight, having had the full treatment off Edgar earlier and not very keen to bowl at him again. With fielders well spread out I bowled a terrible ball — Edgar did not know whether to hit it for six or a four. He must have changed his mind and lobbed a dolly catch back to me. I could not drop it, although I wish I had done, because to the best of my knowledge, as good a bat as he was, he never made 100 in an innings in the whole time he played.

Another character in village cricket was Stan Preece of Knockin Seconds. A left-hander, he always wore a little cap too small for him. The agreement I had with him was that if I was bowling I was to give him a full toss down the leg side. He was manager of Rogers & Jackson, the Ironmongers in Oswald Road, Oswestry, and at that time quite a few of us who had not long been married would go to Rogers & Jackson for a new grate or other household equipment. 'See Stan,' was what I would tell them. 'Tell him you know me.' As I was in the iron trade I was allowed a bit of discount, which he would give them, but only under the terms that he was to have a couple of full tosses down the leg side when we met. The barter system! Or the blackmarket system! We had a bit of discount, Stan his full toss. This worked well for many years until a Saturday when the match was quite close. Stan was to come in to bat. Only one or two of our players knew of the arrangement. 'What shall I do?' I asked Jack, the wicket-keeper. 'The usual,' he said. Stan connected twice. He had his quota. He knew he would get no more favours that day, nor would he expect them. One of our younger players I think had guessed what happened and with a sarcastic remark said to me: 'That is no way to play cricket.'

'It's the way I play,' I said, 'And if you get half as much enjoyment out of your cricket as we older ones have, then you'll be lucky.' I am grateful to Stan for those happy 'bowling and dealing' memories. The last time I saw him was in hospital minus both legs, but still smiling as I bowled him an imaginary ball up the ward. A true cricketer who really enjoyed his cricket. So did Johnny Jackson, who kept wicket for Knockin Seconds, whose appeal for a catch behind could be heard for many a mile. (George Duckworth of Lancashire in the thirties wasn't in it).

Les Jones (Pongo) arranged a knock-out at Cockshutt on Harry Pratt's field at the back of the Red Lion and the Crown pubs (they are next to each other). Now as wicket strips go, this truly was a classic pitch. You didn't know whether to duck or jump, so unpredictable was the bounce. You could come away with a bump on your head and a swollen ankle with consecutive balls, but undeterred, Pongo soldiered on, running the knock-out for church funds. We were to play against an Army side. It had rained non-stop for two days and nights and on the day of the match it was still bucketing down. Surely we could not play. We rang Pongo at about six o'clock to enquire as to the state of the pitch, and to ask when we could play again. 'Where are you now?' he asked. 'We anna started,' I said. 'Well get a move on,' he replied, 'The Army team is here waiting for you.' 'But we canna play cricket in weather like this,' I said. 'What's the matter with you?' he demanded. 'The sun's bin shining here, get a move on and be here in half and hour.'

We piled into two cars, eleven of us, — (like the two drunks, — nobody knew who was driving) and away for Cockshutt, a distance of about seven miles. The nearer we got to Cockshutt, the bigger the puddles. They had had more rain than Frankton.

Les Jones was on the car park in wellies and a mack on. 'It wanna rainin' when you rang.' It was no use arguing. We were to field first in macks, some wearing trilby hats, trousers rolled up almost to the knees. I don't think even John Arlott could have found words to describe the sight. 'Got any sawdust?' asked Tony Jarvis. 'Some coming tomorrow,' said Les. 'Some bloody use tomorrow,' called out Tom Goodwin.

We only played ten overs a side. What the result was I canna remember, all I remember is that we were all like drowned rats. After changing and in the Crown, Les asked if we had enjoyed the match — I dare not repeat our reply. 'Ah, well,' he said, 'If you had na come, you woudna be 'avin a drink so early.' (The time was only about half past seven — his Mother was landlady at the Crown).

Bowling one evening in the Cockshutt Knock-Out, Peter Done appealed for l.b.w. with each of his first four balls that he bowled. With his fifth ball came another loud appeal. The umpire said: 'Dunna shout so loud, lad, you'll make me lose my count.' The umpire was more concerned with counting the pebbles in his hand as every ball was bowled than to Peter's appeal for l.b.w. He wanted no seven ball over for the likes of Done!

I write this in Frankton's first Pavilion. It's an old railway cor -

tainer which I bought off Frankton C.C. when they had their new pavilion some years ago. I have just come up from beloved Hardwick Park. How well it looks with its outfield mown as short as a lawn, the pavilion on one side and Hardwick Hall standing in all its splendour on the other. What a true English country scene — none better in the whole world, — in my world at least. A setting that has stood for years and one hopes will for many years to come. One's mind goes back to the start-up of Frankton Cricket Club again after the war. Changing behind the gorse bushes, tea in the stable yard, the tea ladies waving the table cloth to summon us down to tea.

Then we progressed and bought a tent which had to be put up and taken down at each game (was it progress, or just harder work?). Then the old railway container, which I now have at my farm, arrived.

We didn't have the outfield until the end of July. The cows grazed up to the square. The ball had to be hit in the air to score many runs. Many a four was cut off when the ball disappeared in a ruck of cow muck and many white flannels needed a good clean after a slide along the boundary. Frankton Cricket Club has come a long way since those balmy days just after the war. To think that one day, Frankton Cricket Club would have two sets of covers to cover the wicket! Truly a far cry from the days when we had to go for a pee behind the gorse bushes. But are they as happy I wonder?

'Barney' Jones was driving us to one match with Ted Timmins sitting in front with him. Jack played his party trick on Ted. The steering wheel of its wagon was held on by a $\frac{5}{8}''$ square nut. Jack had loosened this nut so he could remove the steering wheel quite easily. As we were going down the brow, he said to Timmins: 'Do you want to drive?' and handed him the steering wheel. I don't know what Ted's reaction was but Jack played that trick on so many unsuspecting people on later trips. How he kept control I never did know. I believe he once did it to a council official, Dick Cope, from Welshampton. Dick was telling him to slow down. Jack handed him the wheel and said: 'Drive the bloody lorry yourself!' Jack was also a very keen motor cyclist who used to compete in motor-bike races held at Park Hall Camp before the war. Also, he went to Whit Monday Sports when 50 miles an hour would have been a terrific speed.

135

Mention of motor-bike racing at Park Hall Camp reminds me of how as kids we used to sit on the grass verge by the finger-post on Good Friday morning before a race. About a dozen of us used to have different registration letters to count. The first to twenty won, then we all started with different registration letters — AW, NT, UX, JU were the most popular letters, all being Shropshire. Most still had only two letters. AW and NT were getting out of date. We would also count the number of push-bikes that went past in the hour, not that many in a year now. I have already mentioned the playing of marbles on the main road on the way to school, and running with bowlers (hoops), tops and whips. Now you hardly have time to cross the main road at a run.

One Saturday afternoon, Frankton Cricket Club were playing Knockin Second XI. A parson, the Revd. R. C. Roberts was playing along with his brother, I'll call him John Roberts, both being in their sixties and requiring a runner each. Brother Bill was bowling to the Revd. Roberts who connected. In the confusion that followed, somehow or other, both batsmen and both runners arrived at the same end. Arthur Jones, threw the ball to the end where the four were stranded. Like a shot out of a gun all four tore off for the other end. Jack, who was the wicket-keeper, threw the ball to Roy Walker, who broke the wicket and appealed for a run-out which was granted. But which batsman was out as the four of them were about halfway down the wicket when it was broken? A friendly argument started between the parson and his brother as to who should go out.

Brother Bill suggested they should toss for it. The Revd. Roberts said, being a man of God, he would not resort to gambling by tossing a coin. 'However,' he said, 'I have made a decision. As I am the elder brother, my younger brother is out.' No more arguing and out his younger brother went with his runner. That could only happen in Frankton.

I never could bowl well against Whittington Second XI, but one Saturday, I was having a bit of luck with two or three wickets. Davy Goff, who was playing for Whittington at that time shouted: 'Alf, your wife has just sent a message. Could you go home as your cows are all out on the main road.' Village cricket humour at its best. Ken Evans from Alberbury came in to bat once, — brother Jack was wicket-keeper, brother Bill was umpire, and I was bowling —

136

Ken looked first at Jack, then at Bill, then at me, and remarked to Brian Foulkes, the batsman at the other end: 'What bloody chance have I got if the ball hits me on the pads?' 'None at all,' said Brian, 'None at all.' As if we would dream of such a thing, — or even water the wicket one end of Hardwick Park!

Doug Gough was playing in that match, — a better bloke never graced a cricket pitch, but he wasn't much use in the out-field. A bowler who didn't know this put him there. The batsman skied a ball. To everybody's amazement, Doug brought off the catch of the season, only to see the umpire shake his head.

'What do you mean?' asked Frank Bailey. 'I mean NOT OUT,' the umpire shouted back. 'One of his feet was over the line.' How he could see that from behind the bowler, nobody knew. Poor Doug! One time in his career to be 'man of the match' thwarted by an umpire with a pair of binoculars!

137

Chapter 19

'Borrowing An Umbrella On A Fine Day'

A BIG decision was taken at about this time in my life, to have a *telephone* installed in the house to help me run my business. I had also progressed to a better car, a four door Morris-Eight, complete with running boards, too! A telephone was quite a major decision and so was a four door 1938 Morris-Eight. It was a major step forward in our status as a family and opened up a new world, able to ring up any where in the world from your own fireside.

My Mother had brought her old home at Tetchill, and had moved leaving Frank and I to look after ourselves; Jack had moved with her (he looked after her, better than any trained nurse could have done).

Tommy Atkins, a local Auctioneer, was asked to value my Mother's farming stock for me to buy, as I was going to continue on with the small-holding of 22 acres, as well as the village smithy. I had been on my bike to see the then Major Kynaston, the landlord, who had returned from the army to run Hardwick Estate (he had been away from 1935 to 1950). He agreed I could have the tenancy. At the time he was living in Hardwick Lodge prior to moving back in to Hardwick Hall.

Tommy Atkins came, nattily dressed with cap tilted at a jaunty angle on his head. Note book and pen at the ready he valued Mother's 9 cows, 2 heifers, 2 yearlings, 3 calves, 1 sow, 50 hens, milking stools and buckets, and a few small tools. (No ponies as Peg had already died and my Uncle Jack had bought Nobby off Mother). I was going to have to buy a tractor of some sort or other, later.

After the valuation was complete we went into the house for the inevitable cup of tea and piece of cake. I was dying to know what sort of valuation had been arrived at.

I asked Mr. Atkins; his reply was: 'You will get it officially typed in the post tomorrow. But, if your Mother will allow me I can give you a rough idea in five minutes.'

'That will be perfectly alright by me,' said my Mother. I waited with bated breath, knowing that Mother had to have as much as possible to help Jack and her to buy her old home at Tetchill, but also not to be too hard on me, because I was the one who had worked at home for the last ten years for a low wage.

After what seemed an eternity, Mr. Atkins said that in his opinion the valuation to be fair would be £529. My heart missed a couple of beats. Where on earth, I thought, am I going to find that sort of money. Mother broke the silence, with a remark I shall remember for the rest of my days. 'With you as witness Mr. Atkins, if Alf can find £200 I will wait a bit for the rest. He can start to give me some more, a bit at a time, out of his monthly milk cheque.'

'You know only Mothers can come up with statements like that,' said Mr. Atkins, a remark I fully agree with. Shaking hands and bidding Mother goodbye Mr. Atkins left towards the door. I went out on to the road with him. He shook me by the hand as well and wished me well and away he went; his valuation came through the post a couple of days later, all nicely typed out. I then realised that I had not even got the £200 my Mother needed, let alone £529.

Armed with an Endowment Policy for £100 — on which only one payment had been made, which did not mature for another fourteen years, I went by appointment to see Capt. Brasher, the then Manager of Lloyds Bank in Ellesmere. This was a complete new experience for me, how I wished as I sat waiting I could change my mind and not try to be a farmer as well. My throat felt dry and I thought that everyone that came into the bank was looking at me, but *now* I realise they had their own problems.

Eventually a door opened and my name was called out, 'Mr. Brasher will see you now Mr. Strange,' a voice said from somewhere.

Going into his thickly carpeted office I felt more uneasy than ever. He was seated at his desk with his glasses on, he raised his head and looking over the top of his glasses he said: 'Sit down; what can I do for you?' As I went to sit down, the valuation which I had in my hand fell on to the floor, stooping to pick it up I knocked over the chair which I was supposed to be sitting on. I felt my face go red as a beetroot. I handed him the valuation, he took it and read it for about two minutes, 'What were you wanting?' he asked. (I thought to myself — what does he think I want'). I stuttered: 'Can you lend me £200 to help to buy that stock off my Mother so I can start a bit of farming as well as my Blacksmith's business?'

He repeated, as if I had said two hundred thousand (his carpet was worth £200.) 'My advice to you *young man* is to forget that idea, I feel sorry,' he said, 'For people like you who think they can start farming with no capital.' He rose from his chair and proceeded towards the door. He was not going to give me another chance to put my case; it must have been the shortest interview he had ever had. (Today, the banks seem to be breaking their necks to lend to babies in prams!)

Outside on the street again I thought that was the end of my farming career — stopped before it had started; walking up Market Street a thought struck me — I wondered, 'Will I dare go and ask him?' 'I will!' I thought, and I found myself knocking at Gough Thomas' Office — one of our two local Solicitors. He hadn't a reputation of being a benefactor in most of his dealings, but you could talk to him while you could not at the bank. I was trembling as I enquired of his secretary as to whether he would see me. 'Have you an appointment?' she asked haughtily (I thought), 'NO,' was my reply. 'Sit down and I will see whether Mr. Thomas will see you.' I must have been in luck, for the reply was: 'Go on in to his office.' His office as I remember was very dark and dowdy (no thick carpet for Mr. Thomas, I thought). 'What can I do for you, Alf?' he asked. The 'Alf' was sufficient to stop me trembling. Briefly I explained my needs. I said: 'Could you lend me £200 please?' He had a quick look at the valuation, and to my amazement he proceeded to write me a cheque out for two hundred pounds. 'That will cost you $3\frac{1}{4}\%$ interest,' he said, '£6 10/- a year, go and see Mr. Reade and leave him your insurance policy', — Mr. Reade being his assistant. I shot out of his office before he could change his mind, saw Mr. Reade as he told me to, left my insurance policy with him and then straight back to Lloyds Bank to put the cheque for £200 into my account. This meant I could pay Mother the first instalment on her livestock, so I can thank Gough Thomas for giving me a start in farming. Farmers will sympathise when they learn that two thirds of my milking cows — six out of nine— aborted that first year.

Many more stories of which I have to tell, but on reflection I made one mistake that day, I should not have gone back to Lloyds Bank with that cheque. I should have gone to another bank, because now I had a bit of capital and as the old saying goes — 'a bank will lend you an umbrella when the sun is shining, but when it starts to rain they ask for it back.'

Chapter 20

' Mother Goes Home — I Go Courting '

IT was in 1949 that Mother decided she had had enough of farming her twenty-two acres and bought her old home at Tetchill and moved there with my brother Jack, leaving Frank and me on our own at the Perthy. We lived on our own for the best part of two years, taking it in turn to cook evening dinner (egg and chips was about the best I could manage). Mrs. Prodger who lived at the council houses used to come in five mornings a week for about an hour to tidy up for us, make the beds and such; Gladys from the White House on the Brow would do us a bit of washing as well. Frank was quite a good cook, we used to have a fairly good Sunday dinner even though the custard was a bit thin sometimes. Now, I was the proud owner of a motor-bike, *Raleigh* was the name on it, although I think the name *ABC* — 'all bits combined' would have been more suitable. I bought it off John Humphreys, who lived up the Perthy, for £5, at least that's what I think I gave him for it.

Was this not the machine that he had made in our smithy? He used a bolt out of a round hurdle, a bar of iron to hold the front wheel and the front forks to the main part of the bike, ordinary iron it was, not steel. One day he was coming down the Bank towards the Perthy Chapel; he went to turn the corner only to find the bolt had sheared off, the front wheel went straight on. So did he, straight over the hedge into Wyn Edwards' field. His mother blamed me for letting him use an old piece of iron for a pin!

That is how I came to buy this latest piece of machinery to add to my fleet of motorised transport. I don't think he was 'done' at £5 seeing most of it had come out of the smithy. I was now the proud owner of one car and one motor-bike. Little did I think what near disaster was due to befall me and Vera, my wife-to-be.

We had been to the Garrison Dance at Park Hall Camp. George Riley's Band was playing. To our dismay my car would not start, a push by some soldiers still 'no-go', so we left it in the opening to Tinkers Green Halt, a small little station used mainly by Army lads stationed at the Camp. (Now both closed: what memories that Camp and station must hold for thousands of troops who passed through its gates). A phone call to Burgess Taxis produced a taxi, driven by Miss Benbow. We only booked it to Frankton, we had not enough money to book all the way to Welshampton, where Vera's home was, — another four miles or so would have cost another 5/- or more at that time of night. Had I not got a newly acquired motor-bike? We got to the Perthy walking from Frankton, I suppose at about 1 o'clock.

Starting up, away we went, but, going along the Mereside at Ellesmere, disaster struck. The engine seized up, we skidded violently but fortunately did not crash. After a bit I got it going again. Vera jumped on to the pillion seat as I crashed the machine into gear. I must have let the clutch out too quickly, the bike leapt forward and I swear Vera's feet hooked around my ears, as the engine stalled again. No amount of coaxing and using the kick start, nor cussing could get a squeak out of the bike. Leaning it against the Boathouse Restaurant, I walked Vera home to Welshampton and then faced the five miles home again to the Perthy. Luckily a welcome lift home from Ellesmere with a passing Land Rover came to my rescue.

Vera and I went one night to Chirk to buy a chassis that was on an old Hearse, it had four wheels on but the chassis part was not strong enough for me to make into a hay lorry. The chap who owned it was trying quite desperately to persuade me to buy it. But, no way was I going to part with my hard earned money. 'I'm sorry,' I said, 'It inner no use for what I want, and I can't spare my money to buy it to keep in stock.'

Everything bought in those days had to be turned into money straight away (or earn its keep in another way). 'You know,' said the chap, 'It's the chassis of a hearse?' 'Yes,' I replied, 'But I still dunna want it.' On that his son who I think would be about fourteen years old, and had been listening to our conversation, turned to me and said, very seriously, 'It has not been driven very fast, Alf.'

I don't know what happened to that lad but I have often thought about him over the last thirty years or so.

Our courtship, I suppose, followed the usual pattern of most young people *in those days*, — pictures at the Regal or the Kings in Oswestry, or the Town Hall in Ellesmere, dances at the baths in Oswestry (although Vera always reminded me of the earlier time I should have gone to the baths) or the Garrison, the Plaza, and occasionally Trentham Gardens. Joe Loss and Eric Winstone often played there. We used to go on Tom Hyde's bus, — quite a treat in those days of the early fifties. Dances in Ellesmere Town Hall were very good. The leader of the band was Harry Pickup, — a one-armed drummer. He managed alright, though, with one arm and his two feet.

One morning in Oswestry, our local market town, at a garage I saw a Singer Gazelle for sale. £180 was the price, a real beautiful car she was and I thought, if I can get the owner to give me about £30 for my Ford-Eight — No. BVT 401 (which cost £12 10/- you will remember), I would try to buy it. I could not afford it really, but what annoyed me was the fact that when I asked him, the garage owner, made the very same remark, — that I could not afford it leaving me standing on his forecourt. He never even looked at my old Ford. I never had the chance even to tell him that you started her up with a No. 8 horse nail.

Over the last forty years I have bought many new cars but never one off him. The reason being: I never gave him the chance.

Chapter 21

'Cash Flow 50's Style'

THE system that Dad followed to send out bills, even in 1947, was very much hit and miss. His terms were supposed to be quarterly, but his system was that he would write so many bills out, send us out with them or go to some of the farms himself. If he had a good response from those, that would be it. Leave the others for a few more months.

Then he'd write out another ruck of bills, and that was how he liked it. He said to me once: 'It's nice to have a bit of money out'. (and somehow I have always thought the same way). But of course he knew his customers. They were all friends.

Times were changing fast. Firms who supplied me with iron and other services and materials were wanting their money much quicker. Particularly as I was new on their books. Going was the personal trust of the traveller calling every three months for his order and his money, more so because I was a new account in their ledgers. It was cheaper and easier for them to telephone for an order and to send a letter for payment. I tried hard to educate my farming customers. The young 'uns were not too bad, it was the 'owd 'uns who were lothe to change.

I went to see Bernard Hallett, an accountant who had just started up in Ellesmere on his own. I made an appointment to see him at his office in Trimpley Street, next to the old food office; (it was a shoe repairers, before the war); Seven o'clock in the evening was the appointment time. We both arrived at the same time, on *push-bikes!*

He had his case on a carrier on the back mud-guard, I had my book in a bag on my back! He agreed to do my bookwork for me. I was to do my daily booking, and at the end of every month he would get the accounts ready and the agreement was that he would post them! The system of my taking them was old-fashioned, so he said. I didn't like this idea. I said: 'It wunna work.' His reply was: 'It will have to work. This is money and while you are going round trying to get money in, you could be earning more.' We tried it for twelve months and as I expected, only a very small amount was paid in. I would not allow him to send any demanding letters. I was having enough trouble as it was trying to educate my farmer customers into realising that they would have to pay more for their jobs as my overheads were rising. Inflation was starting, even in our little village. That was in 1948, like sex, it didn't just start in the 1980's.

Iron and other working materials were costing more. A telephone bill was now appearing, — the second telephone to appear on the Perthy! After about twelve to fifteen months of Bernard Hallett's system, which, in my case never worked, we arranged he would get my bills ready for the end of every quarter and I would revert to the old system of taking them out by hand. That worked much better. We at least started to get some money in. Today, it is called 'cash flow'. Some farmers I would leave for about twelve months, knowing full well that I would get paid when I went. One I recall was that I had been to this one particular farm at the previous Christmas, arriving again the following Christmas. His remark to me was: 'Good God, Alf, you was 'ere last Christmas, meithering after money.' I answered: 'Aye, and I will be here, God willing next Christmas as well.' 'I hope so,' he said. 'Come on in and 'ave a drink,' — and he paid me! Country dealing again!

Back to the cash flow business (a couple of years before I would have thought it was something to do with skimming pennies on the Pool.)

In my early days as a blacksmith new expenses were beginning to appear: telephone bills, running a car, rates etc., and village black-

146

smiths were having to start charging at realistic levels to reflect these additional expenses for their labour.

At a meeting of blacksmiths to discuss pricing, one of the older craftsmen asked me how much he should charge for a job. I inquired how many hours of labour he had put into it and his answer was 'I dunna know — but *it was dark when I finished!*'

One evening I called at a farm with my bill (sorry Account — got to talk posh now) it was about 7 o'clock. The door was open, but I could not find anyone about. But I could hear a voice shouting, 'Help me,' 'Let me out.' I stood and listened. The voice was coming from the garage down the farmyard. The door was bolted on the outside. Inside, with the car was the farmer's wife. 'Are you alright?' I shouted. 'Yes,' came back the reply, 'But please let me out.' This I did.

'How on earth did you get fastened in like that?' I said.

'My husband bolted me in,' said the woman. 'We had a row and I said to him that he was not going to the pub in the car. So I came down sat in the car and I never heard him coming. He bolted me in the garage and has gone to Ellesmere on the tractor.'

Whether he would have let her out when he came back, I did not stop to enquire, probably it would have depended on how much he had, he liked a lot.

There was no point in leaving my bill and I don't suppose she was ever foolish enough to sit and wait in the car again.

The farmer was the central character in a few other instances. In Black Lion yard in Ellesmere one night, there was quite a commotion. A little the worse for drink, he had come out of the Black Lion, got into the back seat of his car and was playing hell because he could not find the steering wheel.

He kept saying someone had pinched it, and insisted on someone going for the police. Thank goodness he allowed one of the local lads to get in the front on the pretence of going to the Station. This lad had the good sense to drive him home. He helped him into the house, and drove the car back to Ellesmere, returning it the next day.

It was the same farmer who backed his car into the muck ruck filling his exhaust with muck, so that the engine would not start, he then got the starting handle and tried to clean out the exhaust pipe. The policeman came just at that time, to look at the Movement of Livestock Record Book, and, knowing the farmer, suggested it would be better if he put the starting handle in the proper place, in the engine at the other end of the car.

This reminds me of an incident in a village shop, — not in Frankton, I hasten to add, at the end of the war. Such traders had a hell of a time trying to make a living out of the meagre rations they were allowed to sell. That particular morning, the traveller from the wholesalers had barely got his foot inside the threshold, when the battleaxe of a proprietor on the other side of the counter, started. No 'good morning', — straight in. — 'I'm glad you've come. I've had a very nasty letter from your firm this morning about our Account.'

Without stopping for breath she went on: 'I'll tell you what we do in this establishment, — at the end of every month we put all the unpaid bills in this 'ere draw, opening the drawer to prove it was genuine. 'And I pick one out, the boss picks one, and our young Tommy picks one. We always pay those three, — we never miss. But I'm telling you this, if we get another letter like this,' — she produced the offending document from her overall pocket, 'Your bills wanna go in the drawer.'

The traveller was speechless. Well, there was nothing he could say, was there?

I think some of mine must have missed going into the 'drawer' — but I daren't let that fellow in Ellesmere know, or he would have said: 'What did I tell you!'

Methods were fast changing, bigger firms were wanting their money in before you received their supplies. I once had a letter from a firm whose supply I had only had a day or two before. They had written on the bottom of their bill in bright red ink: 'Alf, have you lost your pen?' I sent a letter back to them without a stamp. I just wrote in capital letter *in pencil* on a plain piece of writing paper the one word 'YES'. They never sent any more letters like that; but the system was changing fast.

Firms were not working on Saturday mornings. Five day week was here (I don't know if it were school teachers or stockbrokers who started it). Orders for materials had to be given weeks in advance. At one time one could ring British Oxygen at Bromborough on Saturday morning and get a delivery on Monday, but change was coming in every way in business. Progress on the farms was making it a rat race, previously rats belonged to threshing days. Farmers were having to run to stand still. 'Production was up, profits down.' How many times have I heard that. 'Who was to blame? You tell me!'

One of the more unusual jobs I as a blacksmith was ever called to do was to make three bars to prevent any of the area's young men gaining access into the maid's bedroom at a certain farmhouse. The room was at the back of the house, bordering on a field, and it was quite easy to obtain a ladder from the stackyard without the farmer or his wife being any the wiser.

After making the bars and fixing them to the window frames with bolts, I thought what a spoil sport I was, so I left an old spanner on the windowsill so that the maid could take the nuts off the holding pins and replace the bars once her visitor had gone. No one ever cottoned on.

Over many years of dealing with horses as a blacksmith I have made a very strong point of stressing to every rider the need to wear a proper riding hat. There is one very good reason for my attitude — an incident involving a young lady many years ago. The lass came to my Smithy on a fresh horse, her father had just bought her. It was quiet enough to shoe, and afterwards I led it out on to the road, helping the young lady to mount by giving her a leg up.

She had just about got on when the horse started to run backwards almost as fast as many can go forward. I loosened the reins and tried to get behind the animal but before I could do so, it reared on its hind legs and the rider came over backwards, landing head first on to the metalled road from a height of about 10 feet.

Fortunately she was wearing a proper riding hat but I am certain that had she not been doing so, she would have been killed.

The lass's name was Joan. Had she perished in that accident she could not have this year have been wearing the chain of office of the Mayoress of Oswestry as Mrs. David Lloyd.

The pony was later found to have developed this bad habit of running backwards under certain circumstances, though perfectly quiet in every other respect. It was quite unsuitable for a young girl and was disposed of very soon.

149

Chapter 22

' "Electricity"—Better Than Elbow Grease '

THE arrival of electricity in our village was quite a revolution, it meant that the smithy fire could be blown with an electric fan blower. A new electric drill was acquired and an electric grinder, the total cost of that lot was about £80. I had an idea where the electricity was coming from, but not where the money was to come from. No good going to the bank — Mr. Brasher was still there. A contact was made through the good offices of Mr. Webb, the Shropshire, Hereford and Cheshire Rural Industries Bureau Organiser (now re-named COSIRA — Council of Small Industry in Rural Areas). He managed to get me an interest free loan for five years to buy them; it worked out that the repayments were about £3 a month.

What a change they made to the smithy, — drilling a dozen holes in iron in less time than it took to drill one by hand; grinding, instead of chisel work; the end of that drudgery of a job, blowing up a fire with hand belows. Then more progress, an electric welder, but its arrival in my smithy nearly caused the calling of a village meeting in the Village Hall.

I had told the electricity board I wanted 3-phase in my smithy, but they informed me that would not be possible due to cost. A certain Mr. Farmer from Oswestry came to see me and said that single phase would be alright for any work that I would be doing, but I don't think he allowed for the arrival of television on the

Perthy at the same time as my welder, and also that Alf Strange, village blacksmith, often worked until about 10 o'clock. As I remember when I struck the arc and started to weld, all television pictures on the Perthy disappeared from the screens!

Mrs. Jarvis and Mrs. Davies came to see me to complain (rightly so).

What was the point of having a welder if I could not use it. So we had to compromise, a bargain was struck that I did not use my welder when *Wagon Train* was on, on Monday nights nor when *The Grove Family* was on — at that time the two most popular tele programmes. Village order and peace was restored and it was not long before MANWEB (the electricity board) put in a bigger transformer and then a second one as well, allowing me to weld and the women to watch their favourite programmes.

I bought an electric motor which meant that with the aid of a bit of shafting, I could run about three different machines off it. I acquired a power saw, a bigger grinder and a bigger drilling machine; the shafting was bolted to the outside wall on two brackets, and the belting which ran off the various pullies was always in the way to get to use my saw; I had to duck under two lots of belting, — quite a hair-raising job, — but it was adequate for me at that time.

A chap arrived one morning with a bowler hat and an official looking book; and asked 'Are you the boss of these works?' 'Yes,' I replied, 'Why?' (My smithy had never been so described before).

He said: 'I am a factory inspector, and I have come to see what machines you are using,' he looked at my set up of equipment and machinery, and I swear his eyes shot a foot out of his head: 'You don't mean to say you use this lot?' he shot the question at me. I replied: 'It's grand, saves me a lot of sweat'. He started to write down in his book all the things that were wrong.

After about half an hour or so, he looked at me and said: 'How many men do you employ in this place?' 'There's only me that works here,' I said. He was stunned. He slammed his book to and stalked away to his car. The rule of the country at that time was, it did not matter if you killed or hurt yourself, as long as you did not do it to employed labour. He would have saved a lot of time had he asked me, how many I employed before he started writing and eye-popping.

The only reason I have for including this story in this chapter is that it happened in the same month. I little thought one morning what an eventful day it was going to be. I had, over the years been able to keep reasonable law and order over the kids who used to wait and shelter in the Smithy while waiting for the school bus, relatively new in our area, needed to transport Frankton children to Ellesmere, due to the closure of our little Church of England village school, — surely one of the most retrograde steps that the Education Authorities have ever taken.

Gone for ever now the village environment for our children. We should have fought harder to keep our school open. Mrs. Groves, the Headmistress, did what she could, as there were still something like fifty-four children going to Frankton school, but alas all to no avail — the Authorities won. If I had known as much then as I do know about bureaucrats of the land, I myself would have certainly done more. If you have time and patience, the system can often be beaten. But you must be prepared to dig your heels in and fight for what you think is right. In my opinion children up to the age of 11 or so should be brought up in their own environment, involving parents, teachers and children. I honestly think much of today's unrest has come about because of the lack of such a system. I must get off my high horse, as this is a book about village life, not about beating the system. But one day, who knows, if I have time, I may write a book about the battles I've had with the Authorities. Certainly in my next book they will get a chapter or two.

Now back to what I had set out to write about at the start of this section. Townies were starting to appear in Welsh Frankton as in other villages — no harm in that, you may say. True, as long as they respected the country code and did not try to change it overnight, as one lad of about the age of thirteen or fourteen thought he could do. The family had just moved in from the Midlands and this lad started to terrify the younger ones of our area.

This particular morning three little girls came in to the Smithy crying their eyes out and it appears that this lad had been frightening them with his brash, tough attitude. I went outside the Smithy onto the road and said to this youngster: 'Behave yourself and leave the younger children alone; fight someone your own size.' The language he used in his reply to me is unprintable.

I have done a bit of cussing myself at times over the years, but what he called me was what I would term sheer filth. With no more todo, I grabbed him by the scruff of the neck and gave him a good shaking in front of all the rest of the children. Like all bullies when tackled he did not like the treatment, and lay down on the road screaming his head off.

The bus came and left without him. I left him still lying down and went back to my work in the Smithy. The lad eventually got up and went back home. Ten minutes elapsed, then into the Smithy arrived the lad's mother; shouting and bawling at me, accusing me of making her son bleed from the ears, the nose, mouth and eyes, and that she was going to report me to the Police and every other Authority she could think of.

I realised that I had to do some quick thinking, or else I was going to be in trouble if she carried out her threats. As she paused to take a breath I said to her: 'Look whoever you report me to, it will come back to me because it so happens *I am the Probation Officer* for Welsh Frankton, as well as village blacksmith.'

For a moment she was struck dumb. The mention of Probation Officer had saved my bacon. I think they had enough trouble with Probation Officers from where they had come. I spoke again quickly, as I had her on the run: 'Go home,' I said, 'And keep your lad under better control, because I shall be watching him from now on.' My bluff worked. No more trouble from him. But it also taught me a lesson, never to take the law in my own hands. Village life as I had known it was fast changing. Gone was the day when the Village Blacksmith was allowed to make decisions on his own regarding the right and wrongs of other people's children.

Chapter 23

' Farming Gets "With It" '

MRS. BARKLEY asked one morning whether she could use our telephone to ring an Ellesmere number. After making the call she asked how much she owed, and I replied: 'Tuppence.' 'What do you mean tuppence? It's only tuppence from Wyn Edwards' and that's half a mile further from Ellesmere than you are.' Trying to explain to someone who has never used a 'phone before that being nearer to the exchange did not make a call cheaper was not worth tuppence so I told her to 'Get on!'

A new phrase was now beginning to appear in village life — A.I. (Artificial Insemination for cows). Other descriptions often used were the 'bull in a bowler' and 'bull boys in bowlers'. Their coming brought a new psychology and a new form of economic planning to farmers and smallholders in little rural villages like ours.

An A.I. centre at Ellesmere Dairies was supplied with semen from bulls at Cheswardine. A telephone call before nine each morning to Ellesmere 252 ensured A.I. Service that day, and meant a cow could be serviced by any breed of bull. For the best milkers a Friesian bull was requested because a heifer calf was desired to eventually replace an older cow. A Hereford would be required for a not-so-good milker, in the hope a Hereford bull calf would be born to supplement the farmer's legitimate income, or for extra back pocket cash! Of course such transactions had always to be declared to the Accountant, though

I once remember our Accountant saying what a bad year it had been for dead calves, some farmers having lost all their bull calves! Aberdeen Angus bulls were in demand to inseminate first-calf heifers so that they would produce smaller offspring, presenting fewer calving problems.

So for about seventeen and sixpence (87½p) you could have the choice from four or five different breeds for your cows including Charollais, Limousins, Holsteins — unheard of names in those days just after the war. I have had many laughs about the messages brought in notes from neighbouring smallholders, brought by the children on their way to school, or while waiting for the bus to pick them up as they were sheltering in my Smithy, after the local school had been so wrongly closed and the village children made to go to Ellesmere (a backward step, in my opinion, for country children as a whole; centralization they called it, but more about that later).

To get back to the A.I. notes. I would open them, and they would read something like this: 'Dear Alf, will you please ring up the Bull Place in Ellesmere and tell them that Nelly, Sally, Mary, or Peggy is a-bulling for the first time and could we have a "heifer calf" or a "Bull calf" as the case might be. Cows had names in those days and were used to being tied up by their necks. Gone were the days when smallholders with a couple of cows or heifers would walk them a mile or so to the bigger farmer's bull. All that was needed now was a 'phone call, a towel and a bucket of warm water and soap. This created a new bearer of news to the village, you no longer had to rely soley on the postman or the milk-lorry driver for news. You could find out off the A.I. boys what was happening in the next village, who was doing what. Sometimes they would say, everybody wanted a Friesian bull because Hereford calves were a poor trade last year, or vice-versa, — everybody going for the Hereford because Friesians were down in price.

Our A.I. man, Phil Morgan, was very helpful in all he did. Farmers are at times a little bit like sheep, inclined to follow one another into commercial ventures, if pigs are a good trade, all go in for pigs. The average farmer works seven days a week if he is milking (or should I now say — when he was milking cows, thanks to the E.E.C.), and they have to be milked on Christmas Day as well. I once said in Ellesmere Market Hotel that if a dairy worker

155

got double money for working Christmas Day, a farmer should get double price for his milk. The sooner politicians realise that agriculture employs a lot of people other than the farmer, and not at the stroke of a pen, decide they do not want so much milk, or beef or pork, the better. Farming is an industry that has to plan years ahead and cannot switch from one product to another overnight. When this is understood, the better it will be for the whole country.

Then cows had names, and one night I had a cow calving in the Pool Meadow along side Hardwick Pool; Norman Birch was with me. After the cow had calved we decided to pop to the White Hart in Ellesmere for a drink, not realising that it was about 10 o'clock. We got into the White Hart just as the towels were being put over the pumps; someone remarked: 'You nearly missed a drink tonight Alf.' Norman, speaking to the Landlord, said: 'Alf has just had an increase in his family.'

Without a moment's hesitation the Landlord pulled two pints and two scotches. 'Well done,' said the Landlord, 'Have those on me, what is it a boy or a girl?' 'A girl,' I quickly answered, drinking my pint and scotch up as quickly as I could. I could not for shame tell him it was a heifer calf that had been born, not a daughter, after he had given us a free drink an' all! The next time I went in the White Hart one of the locals enquired as to how the daughter was. I said: 'If she turns out to be as good a milker as her mother she will do.' The calf was named Alan Pye and for many years a cow of that name was on my smallholding at the Perthy. Alan Pye was the name of the landlord. I never told him any different!

My brother and I were taught to milk by hand, before machine milking had been introduced. In fact I did not have a milking machine until 1954. After our marriage, Vera used ot milk 12 to 15 cows by hand every night. Sometimes we had village lads to help and one particular occasion, Ginger Ellis was helping out.

A newly calved heifer was the problem — she needed two people to milk her, one to hold her by the nose and the other to milk sitting on a three-legged stool with a pail between the knees, the well tried centuries-old method.

One always milked seated on the right side of the cow, because that was the side on which they were trained to expect the milker. Almost invariably a cow would protest by kicking and bowling over

156

the pail and its contents out of your grasp at any attempt to milk on the 'wrong side'.

This particular evening, Ginger was to milk this heifer and took his seat on the wrong side, without any difficulty. Vera, who was milking on the other side of the cowhouse, called out he should be on the other side and Ginger replied: 'I know, but I'm left handed!'

I can add nothing except the comment that animals invariably know when not to kick and hurt young people. It reminds me of an incident at a West Midlands Show in Shrewsbury when every blacksmith in the ring froze in horror as a three-year-old toddler wandered under the belly of a huge shire horse known to be difficult to shoe.

The smiths were petrified, too scared to move, as another little girl, aged about six, ducked under the rails, caught hold of the little one's hand, saying: 'Come on, you're not supposed to be here'. The tremendous collective sigh of relief could probably be heard in Oswestry.

Chapter 24

'Evnal's Thoroughbred'

SOON after Dick Grindley started to work for me I hurt my back while shoeing a big rough horse. The farmer farming Evnal, — about a mile and a half away from the Perthy rang up and wanted a horse shoeing at his farm. So I had to say: 'Right, Dick will be with you at 2 o'clock tomorrow.' 'O.K.,' he said. This particular farmer bred thoroughbreds. Next day I said to Dick: 'Get out to Evnal Farm for 2 o'clock, go on your bike and shoe his horse for him.' Away went Dick at about quarter to two and he should have been back by about 3 o'clock, but it was about half past four when he arrived.

I said: 'Where the hell have you been?' He replied: 'Waiting for the farmer to come from down the field with the horse.' I said: 'He told me that he would have him in the stable waiting for you.'

A week or ten days later, the same farmer 'phoned again, and he always used to say on the 'phone 'How do?' I said to him: 'Not very happy, you kept my man waiting the other day, I canna pay men 2/6d an hour to wait while you ride around the field on your horse.' He never answered, only to say, could I send Dick the next afternoon, same time 2 o'clock, to shoe his other horse! My back was still playing me up, else I would have gone myself. Dick said to me: 'Take me in the car — I bet he won't have the horse in.' 'O.K.' I said, 'I'll do that.' We arrived at the farm; as expected no horse in the stable, I went up to the road to look down the meadows, and about a mile away the farmer was riding the horse we had come to shoe (I could recognise it quite easily at that distance). I whistled through my fingers to attract his attention; half an hour later he came galloping up towards the gate that we were standing by. Before he had the time to say anything, I looked up at him and said: 'Do you know what you want to do? Get up in a morning and get round these fields before this time of the day.' His reply to me was, without batting an eyelid even: 'You've come to shoe me a horse, not to give me a Sermon.' My reply back was: 'You can have the Sermon for free, but I am going to charge you extra for wasting our time.'

Time was a thing older farmers thought you had plenty of. 'I won't pay for it,' he said. We left and came back to the smithy without shoeing his horse. Two hours wasted and nothing to show for it. That night the 'phone went and I don't know whether he said he was sorry or not (If he did, it would be the only time I knew him to do so, he would shout at his men as though they were slaves). He asked me to go out again next day to shoe the horse, and I shod him many horses afterwards, but he never kept me waiting again.

Times were changing fast, gone were the days when a working man was expected to know his place, especially a young blacksmith just starting on his own. One of Mr. Humphreys' horses I was asked to shoe became quite famous, its name was *Happy Morn the Second.* I don't know how many Hunter Chases it won. I believe it was twenty-seven. There was no extra for the blacksmith, — just a bottle of beer if I was shoeing of an evening, perhaps putting front shoes on a two-year-old that was to be sold at Doncaster Sales.

One night I remember, after shoeing about three of them and waiting for another to be caught, I sat down on my shoeing box, and lit a fag. I offered one to one of the farm chaps who was helping out, he took one and put it behind his ear saying he would have it later. The next time I went to Evnal to shoe, the farmer said to me: 'Look, I can't stop you smoking on my farmyard, but don't encourage my men to do the same.' I don't know how he would get on today with the modern farmworker.

One morning I went to his farm and on the yard was a small calf born premature (seven months) still alive although very small. It was a pedigree Ayrshire heifer calf. 'You can have that calf, Alf,' he said.

I think he thought it was going to die before long! 'Thanks,' I said, putting the calf in a bag and placing it into the back of my car. I shod his horse, then came home with the calf. I said to Vera: 'Here's a present for you, a premature calf, half-dead.' She took it into the back-kitchen, gave it some warm milk, and kept it well rugged up. I thought next morning I would have to bury it. But no, when I came down the calf was standing and bleating its head off. We kept her for many years; she had many calves, and always went by the name of Andy, because the bull's name, the sire, was Andy Dusty Millar, and from 1951 to 1967 (when we had foot-and-mouth) we had some of her offspring.

The farmer of Evnal once took three yearling horses (two-year-olds) to Doncaster Sales. One made about £5,000 and one about £4,000. The auctioneer was having a job to get £2,000 for the third. A friend said: 'You've had a good trade with your first two yearlings'. 'But this one is not doing so well,' said the farmer.

Another story of the same farmer, who sold three yearlings for £11,000, back in the early 50s. I always used to put dates down on my bills. I once sent him a bill with a Sunday date on (my own fault, a slip of the pen). He knocked off 16/- saying: 'I never had a horse shod on a Sunday.' I could not argue with him because that was true.

From that day to this I have never put a date on my bills, only the month, so he saved me a bit of writing if nothing else. I also allowed many times over for that one horse! Just to show how man will spend on something and penny save on others — if Ireland 'phoned about having difficulty in getting a mare into foal, he would inevitably reply — 'Spare no expense — do whatever you have to do.' He was one more village character — it was as well they were not all like him, but a good job we had one of his type too.

Another farmer who farmed near me was Sam Reece. He had quite a big farm, about 230 acres, mixed farming it would be called. He rarely bought corn for his stock. He kept his stock off the land growing his own corn. (Silage, what was that?).

At certain times of the year he may have been getting less than a churn of milk a day. But in Peak Production Periods he could well be getting up to 300 gallons, home produced off his land. One day I was welding at his farm, only one churn of milk on the milk stand. The milk lorry driver obviously knew him well said: 'Sam, you ought to send this churn of milk with the postman.' 'Mind your own business,' said Sam, 'I will farm *my* farm as I want to. I owe nobody any money.' (Which I knew was true. Speaking from my experience of taking my own bills to him. I was always paid without comment, on the nail!)

I used to have to fill in the cheque myself and he would sign it, with a small indelible pencil, produced out of his waistcoat pocket. He signed his cheque 'Sam Reece' half way across it. If all farmers had farmed that land as God intended, or the way Sam farmed, there would not be talk of butter mountains, grain and beef surplusses, milk quotas, etc. Sam was a farmer, a farmer of cows, that fed off the land. Not a cow keeper as was fast starting to come on many farms in our part of the country. A cow to the acre was soon out of date, indeed two to the acre and in some cases three was soon to be common place.

Sam used to visit my smithy fairly often, two or three times a week to have various jobs done, and one of the jobs I used to do for *him* was to shoe him as well as shoeing his horse. He used to wear the back heels of his working boots out quite quickly and many is the pair of heel plates that I have made for him and fitted them on to his shoes. He was a fairly heavy user of snuff and I can see him now sitting on an old chair in our smithy waiting for the odd job to be done, or waiting for his heels to be repaired, popping a bit of snuff up his nose and sneezing like hell.

A chore blacksmiths often had to perform was to ring bulls. I was called to do just that for an elderly farmer one day. I had placed the 'barnacles' as the knobbly-ended pincher put in the nose to keep the animal under control preparatory to putting the ring in place was called ,and the farmer holding on to it.

The bull fell on to its knees followed by the farmer when I said (to the bull): 'Get up! You silly old Beggar!' At that the old farmer said: 'Oh sorry Alf' and climbed on to his feet. I quickly explained I was referring to the bull, not him and we enjoyed a good laugh. Cattle crushers and electric fences had not been thought of then.

161

Chapter 25

'Tom Speke — Who Else?'

PEOPLE say to me as I go around various villages and towns that there are not the characters about today as there used to be. I would agree, for as I have said many times, poverty brings out the characters. But now I write about a true country character (as they all have been) but where exactly to start is difficult to decide.

There are so many stories, the majority of them humorous now, but at the time not quite so funny. His name is Tom Speke and he was born on the Perthy, sixty-two or sixty-three years ago, the son of Jack and Agnes Speke. The cricketer and umpire, Jack Speke, his father, had had trials with Everton, and was a very good walker, winning many races in his day, sufficient to get him handicaps when going on other walks (so much delay, to others, as you will understand). He was also a learned man — self educated as were a lot of country people in those days.

He was a great admirer of George Bernard Shaw, and when you went into his kitchen there would be a large book-case full of history books and such. Jack Speke was a good gardener and he farmed three or four acres on the Perthy. He had a habit when expressing his point of view of raising his one hand up in the air (was it not Wyn Edwards, the coalman who said: 'When Jack Speke puts his *both* hands up, it is time to take notice, and get out of the way').

Tom, Jack's son, I have known all my life, we went to school together, played football, cricket on our field; helped one another to harvest, and have lived within a mile or two all our lives. I told a few tales about Tom in my first book.

We had two yearling lambs in our young days, one each, and had trained our dog Bogie to sit on the back of one, and eventually after many weeks of practising, Bogie could really stick on for quite a while even when the lamb went running across the field.

Tom came down one day and said: 'I bet my dog can do that.' 'Go and fetch him,' said my brother Frank, 'And the dog can ride on the other lamb — the longest will be the winner.'

The lambs were by now half grown sheep. Tom fetched his dog, but as expected the dog kept jumping off the other sheep's back. We had a brain-wave. With Tom's help we threaded a piece of rope through the dog's collar and, somehow or other, tied him on to the sheep's back. Now for the race between the two dogs. We started them off but the dog which was tied tried to jump off frightening the sheep because it was still tied by the neck around the sheep's belly.

Away across the field went the sheep d...gging Tom's dog in its wake by the neck. We ran after it as fast as we could, all very frightened that the dog or even the sheep would be badly hurt. We managed to catch the sheep and luckily both were alright. That was the end of sheep racing at Perthy Smithy but whenever Tom and his dog came past that field the dog would always take off for home.

Tom Speke had another dog named Amos, just how many breeds he represented I would hate to guess, certainly more than four or five! He certainly had a fair bit of Alsatian and Bulldog in him, no doubt that's why he was a great fighter, and a first class house dog. Heaven help anybody who tried to enter Tom's house when Tom was not there. My son Alan was about four when Tom says to him: 'When I die you can have Amos'. He was all excited but I told him: 'But Tom won't die for a long time yet.' For the next six months, Alan every so often, would enquire, 'Has Tom Speke died yet Dad?'

About that time Tom's Aunty Nellie was in Oswestry Orthopaedic Hospital, well over 80 years old, and suffering quite a lot. The telephone rang one night quite late, — well about 11 o'clock, — and a voice at the other end enquired whether I would take a message to Tom Speke, No. 8 Higher Perthy. I said I would, then the voice said: 'My name is Sergeant Jarvis, and the message is that his Aunty has taken a turn for the worse, and the hospital would like Tom to know.'

I put the 'phone down, little realising what a night it was going to be for me. I knocked loudly on his door and suddenly the bedroom window, just above my head, opened and out shot Amos' head, snapping and snarling.

Tom was quick enough to hold on to him by a hind leg, like grim death. The height to the bedroom window was less than 7 feet, I have measured it many times since. I fell back a few yards, frightened because of Amos' reputation. Had he got loose I would certainly have been badly savaged. 'Hold on like hell to him Tom,' I said, 'I've got a message from the Police about your Aunty Nellie. She is not very well and the hospital would like you to go and see her.' 'At this time of night,' said Tom. 'How am I going to get there, unless you take me, pal?' He had always called me 'pal'. 'O.K.' I said, 'I'll go and get the Land Rover.' That was the only vehicle I had at the time and it was anything but posh or plush. It had no top, was very draughty and cold for a winter's midnight dash to a sick bed. Tom was dressed and ready when I got back, and jumped into the passenger seat. 'Have you locked the door?' I enquired. 'No need to', said Tom, 'Nobody will dare to go into that house while Amos is there.' Away we went to the Orthopaedic Hospital. By the time we had gone the five miles or so it was just about midnight. Pulling up on the car park I said: 'Now dunna be long Tom, go and pay your respects to your Aunt, but remember I've got to be up at six in the morning to milk before I start in the smithy at eight.' 'Right pal, he said,' and went in the direction of the ward. After about an hour, he re-appeared. By this time I was stone cold, he opened the Land Rover door and said: 'Come on pal, I've got a cup of tea lined up with one of me mates in the boiler house.' 'No thanks,' I said, 'Come on Tom let's get off home, and how's your Aunty?' 'Oh,' he said, 'I anna been to see her yet.' 'You what?' I said, 'I've been here a damned hour and all you've been doing is drinking tea in the boiler house.' 'Hurry up and pay your respects to her, I'm starved to death, and I want to get home.'

After about another half an hour or so he appeared again and got into the passenger seat. I was a bit angry by this time and he was a

164

bit on the quiet side. After a mile or so I said: 'How's your Aunty, Tom?' 'Oh,' he said, 'she's in no pain. I've been thinking, 82 not out is a good score. It's a pity our English batsmen in Australia couldna score that many runs.' Why he should compare his Aunty's length of life with scoring runs, at that moment, I don't know.

Arriving home it must have been getting on for two in the morning. 'You can manage from here Tom,' I said. 'Oh run us all the way home, pal' he said. This meant about another mile because it was easier to go all the way around the narrow Perthy lane, than to turn around, anywhere in the vicinity of Amos (Perthy lane was only wide enough for one vehicle, there were no turning or passing places in those days). Dropping him off by his door before he got out of the cab he said these words, words that I have remembered ever since! 'Pal' he said, 'You are my best pal, I even class you on the same level as Amos, the dog; But, I'll have to knock twice on the door, else the bugger will bite me.' Remarks like that could only come from Tom Speke.

His Aunty died that night, 82 and out, as Tom had referred earlier. She had worked in the cheese room at United Dairies in Ellesmere for sixty-odd years. Her married name was Mrs. Lightwood. I am proud to have been involved in a little of Perthy's history, even though it meant getting starved to death, losing a few hours sleep, and nearly getting bitten by Amos in the bargain.

Amos himself passed on soon after. Tommy is still going strong, so my son, who is now 27, will never be the proud owner of Amos.

Tom lived on his own in his little house on the Perthy after his mother died, but he befriended many old codgers whose circumstances had changed for the worse. One was quite an eccentric, Eucalyptus Owen, we called him. He was a fully qualified Pharmacist who had worked in Rowlands the Chemist in Ellesmere, and use to advise people to take herbs as opposed to the Doctor's Prescriptions. The herbs he grew in Tom's garden. The reason he was given the name of Eucalyptus Owen by the rest of the village was the fact he used to grow Eucalyptus trees from seed. Nearly everybody in the village had one in their garden grown by him. I know, we had one which grew to a hell of a height. It died in that very hard winter of 1976.

One morning there was great excitement on the Perthy, Frank

Ifield, the great pop singer of that age, was coming to live in Frankton; someone had seen a letter addressed to him.

Was it the postman who leaked the news? In any case it was certainly common talk in the village smithy, speculating where he was going to live. Many places were mentioned. Would Frankton ever be the same again? Scenes of Frank Ifield singing in our Parish Hall grew in number and in clarity, what other pop groups would follow him to our village? The Beatles?, The Rolling Stones?, maybe! And then all of a sudden the truth broke out. Mr. Owen had perfected some wonderful strain of Eucalyptus trees and had wrote to Frank Ifield asking him whether he could name this particular tree after him.

How news can get distorted in a village beats me, but I wonder what would have been the outcome had it been true, maybe Frankton would have changed out of all recognition. I, for one, would not like it to change, but feel grateful to Eucalyptus Owen for bringing a little bit of glamour and gossip into our humdrum lives, if only for a few days. My particular memory of him is of his waiting for the local bus in his long black coat and black trilby, accompanied by his big black dog, who used to sit on a seat in the bus and look through the window like a human being.

Bill Edwards, another character, also spent some time living at No. 8 Higher Perthy. His nickname was 'Cabbage' Edwards; he originated from Whittington (the next village to Frankton, the place where Dick did or didn't come from). There are many stories about Bill but my favourite is the one of the raspberries. My brother Jack's garden bordered on to Tom's house and Jack who had his meals with us told Vera one day, that she could have the raspberries that were in his garden if she picked them. This she was going to do one afternoon, but in the morning there was a knock on the door, Bill 'Cabbage' with about 4 lb of raspberries in a basket. 'Would you like to buy them Vera?' he said. 'Alright', she said. 'Jack has given me his, but I can do with a few more,' she said. 'How much are they?' 'Oh give me about three bob a pound,' said Cabbage. Vera gave him twelve bob for them and he went away whistling. Next afternoon Vera came into the blacksmith shop and said to me: 'I'm going to Jack's to pick the raspberries he's given me. I'll be away about an hour, answer the 'phone if anyone rings.' No one rang in the five minutes she was away, she walked into the shop with an empty basket — not a single raspberry had been left. A little bit of honest(?) country ways!

'Fancy buying raspberries that already belonged to you,' I teased, but many is the laugh we have had over the years about that. Every time raspberry time come round, 'Cabbage' Edwards' name crops up in our house, and Vera always adds the postscript to this story, — How Bill said the day he brought them around, 'Dunna tell anybody I'm letting you have them a bit cheaper than anyone else!'

Tom arrived one day, face cut, hands bleeding. 'What on earth's the matter?' said Vera. 'Oh, I have come off me bike on the corner. Me bike skidded on some loose chippings.' Vera ran some hot water, put some Dettol in it and tidied Tom up a bit.

After she had bandaged him and given him a cup of tea she said: 'You want to be careful Tom, and not come so fast around that corner.'

'Aye Vera,' he said, 'but the funny thing about it is that I came off there yesterday and never hurt myself, and today I was only looking to see why I came off yesterday, and I came off again and hurt myself.'

'It could only happen to you Tom,' was Vera's reply.

Tom decided once to go into the car market and bought himself a great big American car, why I don't know, as he could not drive, and had to rely on someone else to drive him when he wanted to go out. The bonnet was as long as a normal sized Motor.

I was puzzled, knowing it would only do about 10 to 12 miles to the gallon. 'What on earth did you buy a car that big for, Tom?' I said. His reply was: 'Pal, when I go somewhere I want to go in style.'

He was completely naive about motor cars, never having driven one; I like the story told by Charlie Butler, his neighbour, of driving him one night. They had not gone far, — as far as Welshampton, — when Charlie realised they wanted petrol and pulled up at Jack Bennett's petrol station; Jack came out, stopped to look in amazement at the size of his motor, and rubbed his hands thinking it would be ten gallons or even more. Out got Tom: 'Two gallons please,' he said; the smile went off Mr. Bennett's face. 'Are you sure you only want two gallons, Tom?' Charlie asked. 'That will do for now,' Tom replied. Charlie told me it just splashed into the bottom of the tank and barely moved the petrol gauge up at all.

For a time Tom was the envy of the whole village. He changed it later and had a Morris-Eight in its place, a far more sensible motor for him.

'Do us a favour pal?' Tom said one morning as he came into my smithy.

'What's your problem Tom?' I asked.

'Well,' he said, 'Me Aunty from Whittington said there's a hen pen for sale. If I buy it can I borrow your tractor and cart to fetch it?'

'Alright,' I said, 'But you will have to get someone else to drive the tractor as I am too busy.'

'Oh that's alright then, I'll get Bob Humphreys to drive for me.'

Bob was a local lad who had worked on various farms and had been driving tractors for years all over the place. The following Sunday morning Tom and Bob decided to fetch the hen pen from Whittington. I had gone out to a lame horse at Gilbert Brown's of Bromley with Ray Austin. 'It's alright Vera,' said Tom, 'Alf said we can borrow the tractor and cart, we won't be long,' and away they went to Whittington.

Come three o'clock that afternoon they had not arrived back with my tractor and cart. They had decided to have a couple of pints at the Boot Hotel on their way home. Coming along by Halston Back Gate a police car was following them, and what had attracted the police driver's attention was the fact that Tom had decided to sit on top of the hen pen smoking his pipe. The police car stopped them and enquired as to who they were and what they were doing out on a Sunday afternoon with a tractor and cart and hen pen? Checking the tractor was licensed and examining the tyres, and the brakes, even the lights, all were O.K., they said to Bob, — 'Watch how you go and away with you.'

Tom then decided to ask a question, and the question was : 'What are you two after, promotion?' He was still sitting on top of the hen pen, while all this was going on. The police came back to the tractor after Tom's remark and one policeman just casually asked Bob for his driving licence. But he had not got a driving licence.

Tom came around on the Sunday night. 'Had a bit of a problem with the police today,' he said.

'Oh,' I said, 'What was that?'

'Well,' he said, 'The nosey devils wanted to know where we'd been, and where we was going, so I just asked them if they were after promotion. Oh, and they booked Bob because he anna got a driving licence. But I'll pay his fine,' said big hearted Tom and away he went.

Next morning whilst I was shoeing horses a police car pulled up in the front, two policemen got out, one I knew, Ken Ledguard. 'Owdo Ken,' I said.

It was the other policeman who spoke first. 'Mr. Strange?' 'Yes, that's me.' 'Are you the owner of a Ferguson tractor registration No. so and so?. Did you let a certain Bob Humphreys drive it yesterday afternoon?'.

'Yes,' I said.

'Were you aware that he was not the holder of a current driving licence?'

'No,' I said .

'Were you aware that he had never had a driving licence?'

'No,' I said.

'Well,' he said, 'I am booking you on a charge of aiding and abetting.'

'Well bugger me,' I said, 'I was only helping Tommy out'

I saw Tom later on that day. 'Dunna worry pal,' he said, 'I'll come to court with you and I'll baffle 'em with words.'

I said: 'You wunna, you stop at home, you have caused enough trouble as it is.'

The summons arrived, John Scot the Solicitor from Ellesmere defended me. 'You plead "not guilty" and don't answer back, just say 'yes' or 'no' to the Chairman's questions.' he instructed me. The Chairman of the Court in Oswestry was a Mr. Campbell, and I still remember his words to me: 'Strange, are you in the habit of lending any Tom, Dick or Harry, your tractor?'

'No Sir,' was my reply (I felt like asking him wasn't he aware of country village life where we all helped one another. A good job I did not because John told me it may have cost me a pound a word for answering back.) Bob was fined £5 and I got £3, my only motoring offence; Tom the instigator of it all did not get any fine at all, indeed did not have to appear, — only Bob and I.

I put that episode down as another bit of country education. Tom and I have never fallen out in our lives and many are the kindnesses and good turns he has done for me over the years, like getting me a Cup Final ticket for the final between Newcastle and Manchester City in 1954, because he had a contact with a Geordie soldier stationed at Otley. The price I paid was taking a load of manure to one of his mates in Beech Grove, Ellesmere. Bartering system again, it works well! (I drove the tractor myself that time!) I often wonder, when my mind wanders back to those days whether the Newcastle United players knew they had got a supporter all the way from Welsh Frankton (just to confuse them) in *Shropshire!* I've supported Newcastle ever since they won the Cup in 1931 (in spite of the disputed goal!) In the 1954 final, which Newcastle won, I went down to London with John Clay, John Elder and Doctor Elder, in John Elder's new Ford car.

I believe I was the only Newcastle supporter in the Manchester City end that day, at least I was the only one who cheered when Jackie Milburn scored in the first few minutes of the game off a Len White corner. Above I have mentioned the three I went down to Wembley with, the two Johns were farmers, the brother of John Elder was a Doctor in practice. He is about 5ft. 4ins., and a calm professional gentleman, until he gets on to a football enclosure. Then he is a changed man, — directing every kick of the ball with his voice, his arms and his feet, — ready to take on any opposition. Sometimes, we would move away from him, so the crowd wouldn't think that he was with us!

I feel myself lucky to have lived at the same time and place as Tom. Both of us I suppose have been fortunate to have lived in Welsh Frankton, on 'Perthy Patch.' Tom and I share wonderful memories from school days right up to now. My life has been much richer for knowing him, 'Keep going, "pal", long may you live.' My later memories are of him taking his dogs for a walk through Ellesmere, or were they taking him?

One more story about Bill 'Cabbage'. He asked Jack for a few apples off his tree, Jack gave permission. He selected six of the best and took them to a flower show, — and won first prize. I wonder if Tom had put the idea into 'Cabbage's' head?

Chapter 26

'A Few More Village Characters'

I DON'T remember 1922, but I've heard the story often enough. It was on a very hot day in June, 1922 and my Mother's brother, Jack and his mate, Len Nunnerley, both bricklayers on the Hardwick Estate, called at our home at the Perthy for a drink of water before going back to the Hordley part of the estate, about three miles away. Mother gave them a cup of pop each instead of water, and a bottle to take with them. The two men stopped talking a little longer than they should have, and decided to go to Hordley the back way, down Lower Frankton. As they went on their bikes down Lower Frankton lane they rounded a sharp corner and there was a farmer's wife crossing the road wearing no more than a bathing costume; she was going to the canal just in Lower Frankton.

Uncle Jack said they did not know who was most embarrassed, the farmer's wife or them. Len Nunnerley summed the situation up in a single sentence. He pedalled like mad another twenty yards or so, got off his bike, leaned against the gate, watched the farmer's wife going down the field in her bathing attire, and then in a husky voice he said to my Uncle Jack: 'Give us another drink of Emily's pop, Jack.' I wonder how much pop they would drink today if they saw the same girl in a modern bikini? This must have been Frankton's first 'Peep-Show'.

Tragedy hit our little village on another very hot day in the late thirties. I believe it was the summer before the start of the war. Tom Jenkins, the gamekeeper on the estate, was cleaning out the ditches in one of Hardwick woods. He had taken a bottle of tea with him to work and also a bottle of wasp poison, in identical bottles. Somehow or other he mistook the bottle of poison for his bottle of cold tea and suffered the consequences.

It was a terrible tragedy to happen to a young man, leaving a wife and daughter. The Coroner brought in a verdict of accidental death and adding that poison should never be kept in unmarked bottles. I thought at the time that was not much comfort for his family. In a small village, like ours, such an incident shakes the very soul of everyone in the place.

One day my brother Bill decided to pretend to be an auctioneer and to sell one of Dad's cows to a gang of us kids, on the Perthy yard. I can see him now, standing on an old box and enquiring of his audience: 'Who'll give me twenty-one pounds for this lovely cow?' and Tom Speke said: 'No, I won't, but I will give you twenty guineas!'

Perhaps more amusing still, but some years earlier, we were playing at 'Farms'. Jack went into the house first, covered in muck. Mother started to create (she never swore, I never remember her to do so): 'What on earth have you been up to lad?' 'We've only been playing farms, Mother.' (She never allowed us to call her 'Ma' or 'Mum' or 'Mam'). 'Dunna clout me Mother, — I was the pig and had to roll over in the muck heap.' — 'No don't Mother, wait till you see our Bill.'

'Bill?' questioned Mother, 'What was Bill, if you were a pig?'

'He was a hen Mother, and had to lay an egg. He's in a 'eck of a mess.'

Another feature in the country scene that seems to have gone after the war was the regular appearance of the 'Gentlemen of the Road' (tramps) or 'Milestone Inspectors'. They would regularly walk through our village, from Morda to Whitchurch, or the other way about. I believe they were only allowed to stay at Morda Workhouse for a fortnight and then Whitchurch for the same length of time. You could get up to a dozen some days, calling to ask for a mug of tea and a piece of bread.

I believe there was some kind of mark left on gates to show

whether there was a welcome or not. I never heard of Mother turning anyone away. Some would have a few bits and pieces to sell, like elastic, buttons and needles and threads; the exceptional one would make baskets out of reeds.

I knew every milestone from Ellesmere to Whittington, each one was in the hedge bank telling how far it was from town to town. In our particular length of main road there was a stone every mile, first from Ellesmere was at the Nursery, then one at the bottom of the Brow; one just below the Church; one just past Kempster's; and another by Halston Gardens. They were pulled up in 1940 when an invasion was expected, perhaps that is why the 'Milestone Inspectors' disappeared! Like other old country things, — they passed away never to return — all on account of Mr. Hitler.

My old boss, Dave Evans, (who recently passed away), reminded me that I had missed out a couple of stories in my first book about my Granny. One was the day she had the Vicar to tea and as a special treat, had provided some tongue. The story goes that she said to the man of the cloth: 'There you are Vicar, I have got you a nice little bit of tongue.' 'Dear me Mrs. Strange,' was his response 'I cannot possibly eat anything out of an animal's mouth.'

'Quick as a flash my Granny said: 'Oh, in that case I'll boil you an egg.' I think that was the one and only time that particular Vicar ever came to tea.

Another time, my Granny was bringing home from Ellesmere a ruck of medicine in various bottles from the Doctor's, — about a dozen I believe she had — in a basket in the bottom of her old cart. Halfway home a thunderstorm descended, washing all the labels off the bottles of medicine. Arriving home at the Perthy, Granny dried out all the labels in front of the Smithy fire and put them back as she thought was right, on the various bottles. Then her daughter, my Aunty, was sent to deliver them to the various cottages. Two days later she must have thought what she had done. So she sent her daughter to see how the people who had taken the medicine were getting on.

Mrs. Jones answered at the first house. 'How is Mr. Jones going on?' said Aunty. 'Oh', said Mrs. Jones 'He is a lot better. The Doctor changed his medicine and he anna been so well for years.' The reply from another house was that 'They had an increase in the family.' But I don't think they put that down to the change of medicine!

John Beech was a boat builder on the side of the canal down Lower Frankton, a stretch which sadly has not been in use for 40-odd years, though soon it is to be re-opened from Lower Frankton to Welshpool — providing a possible attraction for the new Welsh Frankton 'family week-ends'. The cost will run to millions — maybe it should have been kept open and the cost of repair might then have been only a fraction.

Or perhaps if the Powers-that-be at that time had read the piece of poetry written about 1937 by my old school boss Clayton Jones:

'They tell me they dunna do too well,
With Barges on the old canal
Because a cut barge canna hurry,
As quickly as a motor lorry,
So 'Frankton Port' wunna make a fool,
Of Bristol, Hull or Liverpool'.

John Beech, the boatbuilder, was approached one day by a couple with a boat in a very poor state of repair. They wanted it made safe so they could go touring on the Norfolk Broads. John Beech said he required a couple of days to work out a price.

On that the man said: 'Could you give me a rough idea of the cost?' Eyeing the boat over for about five minutes, John said: 'Somewhere in the region of £20.' 'Twenty pounds!' said the man, 'That is an outrageous price, I'm afraid the most that I will pay for repairs will be £10.' On that John examined the boat again and after a few moments said to the owner of boat: 'Yes, I could do a ten pound repair job to the boat. But I want to ask you two questions. The first is, Can you swim?' 'No,' said the owner of the boat. 'Second, can your wife swim?' 'No,' said the man. 'Well, in that case,' John said. 'I suggest you both learn.'

Reminiscing in the Smithy one day with Wyn Edwards, we got on to the subject of how old waggoners would play tricks on younger farm lads. One favourite trick that used to be played was the one with the two gallon stone jar of beer, provided by the farmer, at harvest time. On a very hot day the beer would be either kept in a pond, or in some wet grass to keep the stone jar cool. One old

174

waggoner had the knack of producing in his hand a black snail, saying that it had crawled out of the stone jar.

He would be the only one who never went thirsty all day — No one else could fancy the beer that the snail had been in.

Conversation would turn to the hard times, Wyn telling of the family who were so poor they used to have bread and milk for Sunday dinner. The mother was a proud woman, and after the children had finished their bread and milk, she used to give them a toothpick each and make them sit on the wall outside their cottage, to pick their teeth, so that the neighbours would think that they had beef for their dinner. What a pity Wyn never wrote a book.

Rosie, whom I mentioned in my first book, was married to Tom Payne, and lived down the fields from us at Hardwick, farming about five acres of land. From time to time she would come and give Mother a hand. Tom had been a Butler at Hardwick Hall, and when he returned from service there, the Major let him have the little farm. They kept about two cows, two heifers and two calves and a pony. The pony's name was Polly — Polly Payne, — and many is the ride we lads had on her, taking her back to his house for him, after shoeing.

One day I was taking her back down the big field with Brian Jones and Brian tickled her under the tail with a thistle, — she took off with me on her back, crashing through the corner of the coppice into his field, before I could get her under control, the old man met me and asked me to help him harness the pony up to his cart. We had a hell of a job to get the crop under her tail, and poor old Mr. Payne kept saying: 'What's the matter, Polly? I have never known her like this before.' She was still a bit sore from where the thistle had pricked her. At last Polly was still, and no lasting damage to man nor horse done.

Rosie was a terrific cook, having been in her younger days, a cook on a sheep farm in Australia. I used to love going there for something to eat.

Later it was my job to take the odd calf to Ellesmere Market for them, first by pony and cart and then later in our little lorry. What a pantomime it was. Tom would never sell his calves until they were about three months old. Although quiet for him, they always seemed to be as wild as the devil when I went to catch them, to load into either cart or lorry. They had two thick sacks tied around them to keep them warm and would kick and bleat when caught. After you had loaded up, into the house for coffee made with milk and a piece of currant cake. Sometimes Tom would want to come with me. He took as much loading as the calf, — a big stout fellow he was!

Lou Ralphs was in charge of the calf pens in Ellesmere auction, and, if you let him have the sacks off the calves backs, would see that you had a good middle-of-sale number.

The house that Rosie and Tom Payne lived in was quite big, and for many years Mrs. Martin of Martins the Coal Merchants, Oswestry, lodged there in her twilight years.

Tom kept ducks, and every night in summer you could hear him calling them off Hardwick Pool. He used to shout 'Wadey, Wadey, Wadey,' and the ducks would come and follow him up the field to the duck pen.

Bob Brunt the policeman, featured in my first book, was looking for poachers one night on the Halston Estate by Whittington. He came across two rabbits caught in different snares. He knew whose snares they were but could never catch the ones who set them. So he took one rabbit out of a snare and put it in with the other dead rabbit so that it looked as if both had been caught in the same snare, a miracle if ever there was one. He knew that sooner or later the man whose snares they were would tell someone in the Boote Hotel about how he had caught two rabbits in the same snare. The temptation not to do so would be too great for any poacher.

Sure enough one night a bloke by the name of Bart was telling his mates how he once caught two rabbits in the same snare. The look on Bart's face when Bob told him that he knew which particular field this event had happened was well worth seeing.

Chapter 27

'Vera — Wife, Cook, Milker, Secretary'

SEPTEMBER 15th, 1951 was I am sure the most important day of my life, it was the day I got married and made Vera Williams from Welshampton, Mrs. Alf Strange. She is a true country lass who had been working in the Egg Packing Station at Ellesmere. Of all the decisions that I have made in my life, this was the best. My life up to getting married had followed the same pattern as most lads of my age, dancing every Saturday night; billiards and snooker in Frankton Parish Hall, the odd night in the pubs of Ellesmere or Whittington; dart matches in the smithy for the Championship of Frankton.

Weddings in the fifties were still quite austere, not like the grand occasions they have today with another party or disco at night. Many families held their reception at home and catered for themselves.

We decided to make ours as 'grand' as possible. We hired Welshampton Parish Hall and nearly one hundred guests were invited. Whenever there is a wedding in a village, friends and neighbours rally round with offers to help, ours was no exception. Mrs. Oliver Davies next door and Mrs. Frank Thomas from Oakleigh Farm volunteered to make the salads. Mrs. Fred Thomas and Mrs. Walter Davies made the trifles. Vera's mother boiled hams and tongues. Two of Vera's friends, Frances Thomas and Joyce Davies, decorated the Parish Hall. There had been sheer panic on the Friday afternoon when they went to dust the chains down. They found the hall in a shambles, workmen were building an extension on to the side of the hall, there were tools and planks of wood everywhere, shavings covered the floor. How on earth could we hold a wedding there!

The workmen were sympathetic and promised they would clear the mess up. This they did and the girls were able to go ahead and decorate the room and lay the tables. My Mother gave some fat hens and cockerels. I took these up to Vera's home a couple of days before the wedding for her and her parents to pluck, dress and cook. I took them in an old wooden crate and placed them in the backyard and went indoors. Returning to the yard with sleeves rolled up ready for a marathon plucking session we found the lid of the crate had become dislodged and the hens running all over the neighbours' garden.

My Uncle Tom lent my brother Jack his best Rover car to take me to Church and to fetch Vera. Frank, my best man, and I nipped into the Sun at Welshampton for a quick drink to steady our nerves. Jack was putting the ribbons on the car ready to fetch Vera outside her house. Then the expected happened, the best Rover would not start.

Panic! Ribbons ripped off and put on to sister-in-law Winnie's car, a Morris-Ten — so there was no ride in a Rover for Vera — but she arrived on time, complete with the bouquet of red carnations made by Levi Jones, a local florist, that had cost the then large amount of £1.10s. The bridesmaids' posies she made herself, using sweet peas given by Mrs. Bill Allman, worked through some silver doilies. Frank and I were dressed in black jackets and pinstripe trousers — suits that had done previous service at my elder brother Tom's wedding many years before. And Vera's 'something borrowed' was in fact her wedding dress!

We had five bridesmaids, one was one of Vera's workmates at the Egg Station, Hazel Griffiths. Another was Avery Lawton of Liverpool, who spent four years of her childhood at Vera's home evacuated to Welshampton. Both were dressed in pink and lilac and the three small bridesmaids, all nieces, were Sheila Strange, Susan Strange and Ann Williams, each dressed in white gowns with blue bows.

It was a Saturday morning; 11 a.m. precisely when I took a bride. Vera Williams took me for better or for worse for the rest of her life. We were married in the morning because most of the younger male

guests were playing football in the afternoon — much more important TO THEM than a wedding.

Vera's mother, with the help of neighbours, laid on a lovely
spread — though still at that time some things were in short supply.
The wedding cake cost £3 10/- and the Vicar, the Revd. Ronald
Egerton, charged 7/6d — giving it back as a wedding present.
Stanley Egerton of the garage played the organ, and he waived the
charge too. So we were doing it all on the cheap! How times have
changed — even 35 years ago the 'give and take, help one another'
attitude still prevailed, though times were changing fast.

The wedding breakfast was a credit to all concerned in those still
austere days of the early fifties. To have a 'do' in Welshampton Parish
Hall was something grand, as many village girls' wedding receptions
were held at their own homes, in the parlour. Today the best Hotels,
for about 150 guests followed by a night-time disco for another 200
or so is the vogue. Thus back to the old arguments, — are they
happier days? Indeed are they as happy even if the whole day is
recorded on a video to boot?

I nearly forgot about my Mother's new dress for the wedding.
After some persuasion she agreed to come, — she had arthritis very
badly, and seldom went out of the house, (she used to sit by the
telephone and pass her time phoning one of her lads or their wives).

'I'll have to have a new dress,' she declared. I had to go to Mrs.
Eric Jones, her friend, to ask if she could take her to Oswestry. She
could, and she did. There was no 'yellow peril' along the streets in
1951, but on either side of Wilson's, the dress shop, the Police had
stuck a traffic pyramid, to stop people parking. However, it was
essential that Mother got as close to the shop as possible.

In she went with a struggle. She came out fifteen minutes later,
just as a Police Officer was getting out his notebook, — now my
Mother was always one for tipping and ever since I can remember
she would give not less than half-a-crown (how she managed it, I
never knew). Sensing the trouble and forgetting it was Oswestry and
not Frankton, and 1951 not 1941 (bear in mind, the last time she
had been in Oswestry would have been with Peg and the trap), she
made no more ado, opened her purse and produced the half-a-crown,
which in her view settled all. The driver of the car had to snatch
the money from her, otherwise as sure as eggs, they would have been

179

up for bribing an Officer. The P.C. let them go, when he saw my Mother's condition. It was a bonny dress by the way.

We spent the whole four days of our honeymoon with Vera's Aunty at Chelford, near Knutsford; we would have a nightly drink at the Dun Cow Hotel at Ollerton; a day trip on the bus to Buxton; a visit to the Cat and Fiddle; a horse show at Altrincham, and then home to Frankton.

Not another holiday were we to have for eight years and that was to be a week in Joe Butler's caravan (the racing fireman) at Towyn near Rhyl. More about those days in my next book.

Soon after Vera and I were married, Albert Roberts said he was looking for a small plough his horse could pull to cultivate the garden. After several inquiries had not borne fruit, his brother-in-law, Harold Edwards, who farmed with his Uncle, Sam Reece, at Hardwick, suggested I convert an old shire horse dragging plough he had on his farm. After drawing up several blueprints, I eventually started to make the plough into a much smaller version by shortening the beam, making the mole board much shorter, and taking about two feet off the tails, as holding handles are called.

We eventually produced a much smaller machine and after a trial run or two with it at Reece's farm, Albert fetched it to his house at Llanforda. It worked quite well. The question arose of how much to charge for the plough. After discussion, it was agreed the job was worth a couple of geese, one for Harold for supplying the original plough and one for me for converting it to a garden plough.

'Agreed', I said, 'But can I have mine for Christmas so that I won't have to buy one for my first married Christmas?' It was delivered a day or so before Christmas, dressed and oven-ready. Would the oven be big enough was our first concern when we saw its size. Luckily it just fitted in the oven part of our old fashioned black-leaded grate. It had a boiler on the other side, which Vera used to polish daily. Microwave ovens had not even been invented then!

Vera's Mother and Dad were supposed to join us for our first Christmas, but her Dad was not too well, and they could not come, so we had this 15-pound goose all to ourselves. I have never in my life been so sick of the sight of goose. Warmed up for dinner, cold on a butty for tea and supper.

Telling this story to George, our vet, he said we ought to consider ourselves lucky, for in his early married days, he was promised a chicken for Sunday dinner when he attended a sick cow on a lady's farm on a Thursday. He told her he would come again on the Saturday. 'You do that,' she said, 'and I could give you a chicken for Sunday dinner.' That was a luxury in those very austere days, and accordingly George told his wife not to bother buying anything for Sunday lunch.

After tending the cow on Saturday, he went to the house to see the lady. He was able to report its condition as 'Much Better', and inquired about the chicken she'd promised, and she replied: 'That's much better too, it lived.'

He could not remember what they had for dinner that Sunday, but there were no deepfreezers, convenience foods, or pub lunches in those days.

Our first child was born on June 1st, 1953, in Oswestry and District Hospital; a day before the Coronation of the Queen. I went in to visit at night like I suppose many others had done before! I saw our new baby a bonny little girl. How proud I felt, it is a feeling you can't express, seeing your first born lying so peacefully in a cot amongst all the other babies, — some crying and some peaceful. That night I had a few drinks with my mates and then to bed.

Although it was Coronation Day the next day I had some hay to turn so I would not be able to go and join in the celebrations until later in the evening, after going to the hospital to see Vera and the baby.

Just as I was about to leave for the hospital the telephone rang, it was Sister Jones from the hospital asking me to see her before I went in to see Vera. 'What's the matter?' I enquired. 'Your baby is not very well,' was the reply. 'But don't worry we are doing everything possible.'

I saw the Sister at the hospital, she was trying to explain the complications that had set in. I can't even remember what she said, I was too dazed. I was allowed to see the little mite for a minute or two, God how helpless one felt to see the little lass fighting for her tiny life. I saw Vera for a few moments; she was very upset and not at all well herself. We were both sick with worry.

I came home from the hospital, I did not know what to do with myself, so I called in the Frankton Parish Hall. The Coronation celebrations were in full swing, but I could not join in as one after another of the villagers was coming to congratulate me on the birth of a daughter. I was too upset to explain to them that my baby was very poorly, so I came home. I rang the hospital about 11 o'clock that night to be told that there was no change in the condition of the little one and Sister Jones said to me: 'Why don't you try to go to bed, we will ring you if there is any change.' I said: 'Can I ring you early in the morning at say 6 o'clock?' 'Yes,' was her reply.

I took her advice and went to bed. Sleep was out of the question. I was up at half-past five that morning just making a drink when the telephone rang, I knew who was on the other end of the line and what the message was going to be.

The only part of the message that I heard was: 'I am sorry, we did our best, would you like to come in and see your wife?' I can't remember the journey to Oswestry, my mind was numbed. I saw Sister Jones before I saw Vera. 'Don't be too long, we have given Vera an injection to make her sleep,' she said. 'Call and see me on your way out, you will need a death certificate to go to the Registrar with.' That again was a shock. I would have to arrange a funeral for a child so young.

Later in the day I went to the Registrar, he looked at me as he handed me the certificate and said: 'Don't be so down-hearted young man, if it is any consolation to you, perhaps it is as well that the little one died, she may not have been able to lead a normal life, as she had a heart problem.'

I thanked him for his few words. They did not mean much to me at that time though, but on reflection, if the little one had not got long to live, the heartache would have been much greater the longer she had lived. I suppose nowadays Linda Strange would have survived with all the new science and technology that the medical world have at their disposal today.

On my way home I called at Eric Jones, the undertaker, and his wife made me a cup of coffee, saying: 'Leave everything to me, I'll attend to it for you.' Her words were a great comfort to me at the time though I suppose being the wife of an undertaker she had seen it all before.

I was not able to do much work in the smithy, but as my farming had increased, 15 cows had to be handmilked night and morning at

182

Perthy. Friends and neighbours were a big help on the day of the funeral as were my brothers. Vera was still in hospital.

After the funeral, life had to go on, horses had to be shod, cows milked, bills and accounts paid, bank managers kept happy. My farming was starting to increase, as the older people of the Perthy gave up their two or three acres and these were added to my small-holding. I was fast becoming the biggest farmer on the Perthy, with by now 40 acres. As I also had a full-time blacksmith's business, life was being lived at a hectic pace. A tractor had to be bought, a man was employed to help on the farm. There were other changes too, a milking machine eased the aches of tired arm muscles — the arrival of two more children in their turn made family life happily complete.

Everything of course was not to go on smoothly ever after, and in the next book I am planning I hope to tell more, both of the heart-aches and of the joys of the life of a blacksmith and farmer. There were trials of course with the death of my Mother, and tragedy when foot-and-mouth disease struck our little village. For six months then I became a gamekeeper, living very close to nature.

Meanwhile village life went on its way. There were battles with authority, the joys of fatherhood, bringing up two children, closure of the village school and moving to a bigger farm — that was a big adventure, just 100 yards in 60 years! They were years of laughs and good companionship too. There are stories to be told of taking up golf, of the people of this unique part of rural England and of the next generation of this strange family called Strange.

I have not composed the following verses about Frankton and Ellesmere but the person who did has given me permission to include them.

THE VIEW FROM THE CHAPEL DOOR

Pray come with me, a village to see,
Which boasts of houses scarce a score,
It's well worth while, you will agree
When you see the view from the Chapel door.

The view is pleasant far and wide,
East and West with mountain galore,
One is the Briedden, the Wrekin too,
All in that view from the Chapel door.

The Church stands near the top of the hill,
The view from there is rather poor,
It's lower than the Chapel,
So you don't get the views, as you do, from the
    Chapel door.

Behind the Church there's another view,
A fertile plain and hills galore,
Well worth seeing, though not so good,
As the view from the Chapel door.

If you are travelling Frankton way,
Stay and see this view once more,
You'll be repaid for you will see again,
The view from the Chapel door.

ELLESMERE

Ellesmere to many is merely a name
And it doesn't aspire to fame,
It has attractions, if you know
What to look for, — and where to go.

The 'Mere', a sheet of water there
Calm, or ruffled, yet always fair,
In summer's glow or winter's weather,
Never the same, two days together.

Beautiful swans glide o'er the lake
So dainty and white, a picture they make,
While ducks, coots and water hens, many a score,
Are skimming the water or busy ashore.

But on the bosom of the lake,
It pleases some a boat to take.
While patient fishermen sit there,
With baited hooks, the fish to scare.

Not far away more lakes may be seen
All worth a visit from those who are keen,
There's Colemere and Whitmere, Croesmere too,
And several others all open to view.

184

At Ellesmere house, just near the Church,
An ancient fir tree find,
It's said it's been a thousand years,
Many memories it may remind.

The Church is worth a visit too,
With links of days long past.
Crusaders brought back many things,
And which for long will last.

Visitors to Ellesmere are not few,
We welcome many people who,
Love all of nature's wondrous treasures,
Better than gold, or a mad world's treasures.

I was with Bill Hodnett and Ern Edwards up on our field on top
of the Brow one day when we all agreed that the view that prompted
our old school boss to write 'See Naples and Die' was indeed one of
the best in the world, with none finer. Ern, then in his 70s worked
on the same farm, The Broome, for something like 57 years from the
age of 13. He worked for three generations of Batho's and in those
years had seen tremendous changes.

Bill in his turn had worked on various farms in the area and could
recall how one farmer came to him one morning to give him his
orders for the week, as he was going on holiday. After a long list of
duties had been recited, Bill asked, straight faced: 'You anna made
a mistake and decided to go off for three weeks, 'ave you?'

Welsh Frankton to me has been home. I never want to move. My
next move will be to Welsh Frankton Churchyard which I hope will
not be for a long time yet. (But I have me doubts now, following a
recent spell back in Royal Shrewsbury Hospital).

To see Naples and die,
Seems strange to me, somehow
When in high summer one can lie
And gaze from Frankton Brow.